The River Tyne

From Sea to Source

Ron Thornton

To Joan

Best Wishes
Ron Thornton

Acknowledgements

I am grateful for all the practical assistance, encouragement and support from many people who have helped in different ways over the two years that I have worked on this project. In particular I would like to thank the following; Keith Bottomley, Alistair Burrowes, Tom Corfe, Clive Crickmer, Tony Edwards and Peter Heath.

A special thank you to my dear wife Ann for her long suffering patience and continued support. My daughter Wendy provided the practical help that turned the idea into a working project. I also need to thank David and Jennifer at Forum books in Corbridge, who suggested that my paintings should be brought together and published.

Should you wish to purchase signed, limited edition prints of the paintings shown in the book, please email: art@rwthornton.com
or visit our website: www.rwthornton.com

Design: Nick Ridley
Printed by Compass Press Limited
Scanning by Spot On Coloursetting

All paintings © Ron Thornton

First published 2002 by Zymurgy Publishing, Newcastle upon Tyne, United Kingdom

A catalogue record for this book is available from the British Library.

I.S.B.N. 1-903506-03-4

Foreword

For me the North East is one of the most magical places on earth. Ok, you might say I'm biased as I was born and raised there but it is true there is a magic in Northumbria and its rivers, bridges, countryside, coastline, history, castles and most of all in its people.

You won't find paintings of all of the castles and ancient monuments which give breath to the stories of Kings and Prince Bishops in Ron's book but you will find a piece of that magic which we northerners love, in his work. Paintings which capture perfectly the scale and grandeur of shipbuilding and engineering in the home of Armstrong, Swan, and Stephenson, and the beauty which is to be found in both the industrial and rural environments of the North East.

As someone who has strong links to Tyneside and the North East, I found Ron's paintings brought back memories of my childhood holidays in the countryside, on the fantastic beaches of Northumberland, and my early work years on the Tyne in both shipyard and theatre.

Nowadays the North East is a place I return to as frequently as possible to work, to relax and to fish. I hope you enjoy this view of my world as much as I do.

Contents

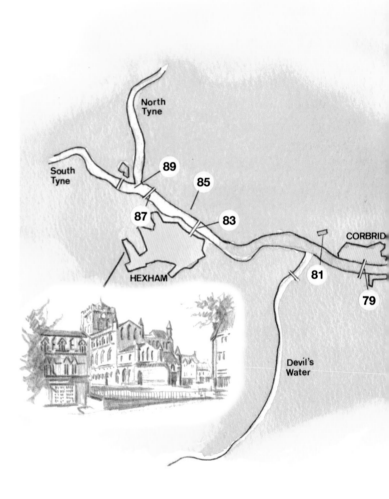

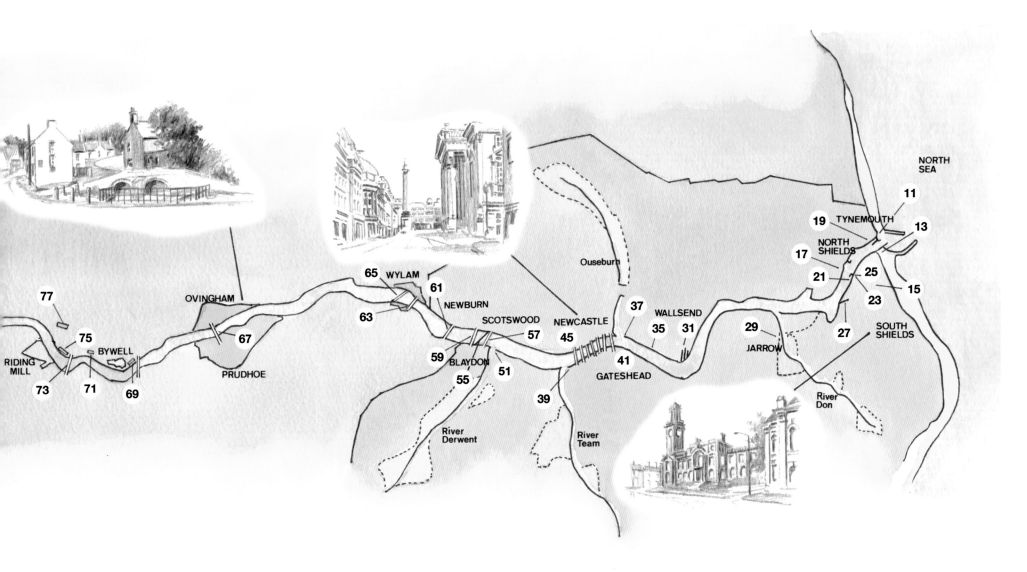

NORTH
SEA

11

19 TYNEMOUTH

13

17 NORTH
SHIELDS

21 25

23 15

Ouseburn

27 SOUTH
SHIELDS

37 WALLSEND

35 31

29

JARROW

River
Don

65 WYLAM

61

NEWBURN

63

SCOTSWOOD

NEWCASTLE

57 45

59 BLAYDON 51

55

41

GATESHEAD

39

River
Team

River
Derwent

OVINGHAM

77

75

BYWELL

67

RIDING
MILL

73 71 69

PRUDHOE

The Tyne

Introduction

Ron Thornton was born in 1936 in South Shields on the River Tyne, at that time an industrial town dominated by shipyards and two coal mines.

Ron has known the Tyne's dirty face and its beauty. Aged forty, he and his wife Ann moved from the grime of the Tyne estuary to the peace and greenery of the river valley and the village of Riding Mill twenty miles away.

At grammar school Ron had shone at art but much aggrieved the art teacher by abandoning the subject to double up at maths. After leaving school he trained as an industrial laboratory technician taking a teacher training college course in order to add to his qualifications and it was at this point that he realised where his future lay.

He progressed to be headmaster of two schools in Newcastle, the first in the city's rough west end with problems of undisciplined pupils from rival estates. Ron brought it to order, "They started off at each others throats but ended up happily integrated and obediently wearing the school uniform" he recalls.

While doing National Service as a radar technician in the RAF based at Sandwich in Kent, Ron rekindled his classroom passion for art by painting landscapes to occupy himself during boring weekends. It has remained a great love of his life and Ron became a professional artist after retiring from education in 1991. He has earned a reputation for his work in oils, water colours, pastels and pen and ink, holding exhibitions in Hexham's Moot Hall and the Old Town Hall, South Shields.

Ron regards the work that has gone into this book as the zenith - and he says - final flourish of his artistic career.

Over a two year period Ron has sketched, photographed and painted the principle features of the River Tyne from sea to source. To research the book he has spent many hours in libraries and museums, village shops and pubs chatting to locals - as well as boldly ringing the bell of a few stately homes - to elicit the facts behind the pictures.

Ron ruefully recalls his closest contact with the river. It was as a teenager when employed as a laboratory assistant who, alone in a small boat, took water depth soundings for the laying of concrete piers to support the proposed Iron Ore Quay - now defunct - at Tyne dock. He said, "Every time a ship sailed past its wash made the boat bob like a cork and I had to hang on for dear life. These days safety rules would not permit such a thing. I could have toppled overboard at any time."

Those who love the Tyne or simply enjoy fine art work will be glad he managed to cling on!

Through a series of paintings and sketches this book celebrates the history, cultural heritage, rural splendour and modern development of the Tyne. The book should interest many throughout the world who have affection and pride in the River Tyne.

The journey begins outside the harbour and follows the river to the confluence near Hexham. From there the course of the River North Tyne is traced to its source at Deadwater Fell beyond Kielder and then the River South Tyne to its origin at Cross Fell beyond Alston.

The art work is supported by anecdotal text that explores the often violent past of the river as well as the dramatic development of the coal trade, the shipbuilding industry and an era of exciting invention involving the contribution of such local luminaries as Parsons, Stephenson, Armstrong and Swan among others. The banks of the Tyne have produced an astonishing number of world-wide 'firsts' which are documented throughout the book.

Preparing 'River Tyne From Sea to Source' has given me much pleasure. The privilege of exploring and capturing the River Tyne in water-colour and pencil as well as allowing me to indulge my long-held interest in boats and water. Along the way I became acutely aware of my woeful lack of knowledge regarding this great river and, as a result of research have become proud of our heritage.

Coal and the Tyne

The coalfields of Northumberland and Durham were first mined by the Romans. Remains of coal bunkers have been discovered in the forts on and around Hadrian's Wall. Coal has driven the economy of the North East from as early as the thirteenth century. In 1592 records show that over ninety thousand tons of coal were exported and by 1800 this had risen to one and a half million tons. Over eleven thousand sailing colliers left the Tyne in 1833 and by 1880 annual coal exports had grown to five and a half million tons. Newcastle became an important centre for industry and engineering.

Coal was carried from the Tyne by sailing colliers known as 'brigs'. These were small wooden, two masted vessels with a crew usually of captain, mate and six hands. Sailors were a hardy breed; they worked with the risk of being wrecked by gales on the rocky coastline. A spell on colliers was considered to be an excellent maritime training school and the navy used to recruit from the Tyne for warships.

On return to the Tyne, colliers were required to anchor midstream to wait for 'Keels' which brought coal down the river. Keels were a type of lighter or barge; the name is derived from the Anglo-Saxon, 'Coel' meaning boat. They were broad, clumsy, shallow vessels that carried eight chaldrons or twenty-one tons. Coal ships' cargoes were calculated by the 'keel load'.

The keelboats were crewed by a skipper, two Keelmen and a boy known as a 'Pee Dee' (no one seems to know the derivation of the name). When the wind was favourable the keels were propelled by a square sail. The main method of propulsion was long oars at each side and a further oar at the stern, which was used for steering. Alternatively a 'pooey' – a long pole pushed into the river (much shallower in those days) was used to punt the boat, which involved the keelmen walking the length of the keel gunwalk from bow to stern. Apparently many keelmen were unfit for further work by the time they reached forty.

It was normal to make use of the tide, journey down river would start at 'slack water' to enable the keelmen to take advantage of the strongly-flowing ebb tide. Similarly, after discharging their cargo, they would await the next flood tide to return up river. The collier brigs had special coal portholes: one forrard, one aft and one in the centre on both sides of the vessel. It was necessary for the keelmen to shovel the coal into the waiting holds. A spare sail was fixed from the hatch cover to the gunwalk of the keel, to prevent coal being lost in the river. The keelmen were paid by the load, with a beer allowance known as a 'can'; the round trip took about twelve to fifteen hours depending on the tides.

On the return journey the empty keel would land at the Sandgate shore, where women known as 'Keel Deeters' cleaned the vessel out in preparation for the next load. No doubt their men folk would enjoy liquid refreshment on the quayside.

Keelers, often called 'Keel Bullies', worked the river from the fourteenth century. Their lives were dictated by the tides and they spent more time afloat than ashore. Their trade was jealously guarded and passed from father to son with few secrets given away. They lived in a close-knit community at Sandgate and usually inter-married. Traditional Keelman uniform consisted of a short blue jacket, slate coloured bell bottom trousers, shirt, a blue bonnet with a flat brim sporting long ribbons, a black silk handkerchief and shoes tied with ribbons.

By the early eighteenth century, sixteen hundred keelmen worked the river using over four hundred keels. Not entirely independent, they had to answer to two masters. One was the 'fitter', a middleman who dealt directly with the colliery owners, who hired and paid the keelmen on an annual bond and provided the keels. He was officially a member of the Company of Hostmen and paid dues to the Crown to secure a monopoly in handling coal cargoes. The other master was the captain of the waiting collier anchored at the river mouth. He considered the keelmen to be a constant source of irritation, rarely around when the winds were favourable and as a consequence little love was lost between the two.

For centuries care of the River Tyne was neglected; in places it was little more than a stream, silted up by indiscriminate shedding of ballast. On occasions it was possible to walk across the river between Newcastle and Gateshead.

Loading at the Staithes

The turning point for the river was the formation of the Tyne Improvement Commission. In 1860 improvements commenced with a thorough survey and six dredgers were brought in to dredge from mouth bar to fourteen miles up river. The two piers were built at the harbour entrance, sections of the river were widened, and two protruding sections of the shore at Bill Point, Walker and Whitehall Point, North Shields were removed. Islands in the river were removed and sections were faced with stone.

The construction of staithes to load coal directly into the holds of colliers was not welcomed by keelmen. They realised that their livelihood was threatened. Violent strikes and pitched battles not only with the police but also with the local militia followed. To make matters worse the Tyne Improvement Commission sanctioned the removal of the Old Tyne Bridge in 1876, which enabled larger ships to travel up the Tyne west of Newcastle. This was the last nail in the coffin for the Keelmen and by 1890 after nearly five hundred years, keel boats were no longer to be found on the Tyne.

For centuries the sailing brigs had undergone little change; they were dependent on wind and the round trip to London on average took a month. The development of the railway network created an alternative route to market. This was countered by the use of steamships. In March 1841, an iron-hulled, propeller-driven steamship 'The Bedlington' was launched into the Tyne at the South Shields yard of Thomas Marshall. She was of a startling revolutionary design. Her holds were lined with rail tracks into which fully loaded coal wagons were placed by means of on-board derricks. Once she was alongside an empty collier, the wagons were lifted out over the holds of the empty vessel, the wagon doors were then opened and the coal teemed into the hold. She also introduced the principle of water ballast held in tanks and holds the proud record of being the first ever iron-hulled, propeller-driven steam collier in the world.

Progress was rapid; the first steamer built specifically to carry coal at sea was the 'John Bowes' built in 1852 at the Jarrow yard of Palmers.

She left the Tyne on her maiden voyage laden with five hundred tons of coal and took two days to reach London, two days to discharge and three days to return. A round trip of a week, compared to the full month required by a sailing brig. Like the Bedlington she had double-bottomed tanks in her underwater section of the hull to carry water ballast. This was easily pumped out at the staithes before reloading. Steam ships brought the demise of the sailing brig, though some continued until the early twentieth century.

The development of the steam collier generated a dramatic increase in coal shipments from the Tyne. Coal was needed for gas and electricity production; in 1911 more than twenty million tons of coal were exported. The discovery of natural gas and the increasing use of oil during the twentieth century brought the demise of coal colliers. On March 20th 1998, the Lord Citrine became the last collier to sail from the Tyne.

R.W. Thornton 2001

Tynemouth Cliffs

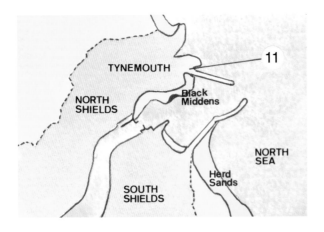

Entering the Harbour

Tynemouth Cliffs offer a platform for the distinctive silhouettes of the Priory, Castle and Watchtower. This rocky headland forms a most dramatic skyline, which for centuries has been gazed upon by mariners with a mixture of emotions; dependent upon whether they were returning home, or embarking on a long sea voyage.

It is claimed that the first Christian King of Northumbria built a chapel on the headland in 627 AD. This was sacked by a band of marauding Danes, massacring a number of nuns who were sheltering there at the time.

The ruins remained untouched until 1075, when they were given to the monks of Jarrow. The chapel was refounded by the Earl of Mowbray after the Norman Conquest. Over the years additions were made until it achieved the status

of a priory. Initially Robert Mowbray had granted the Priory to St. Cuthbert of Durham. However the Bishop of Durham failed to support Mowbray's first rebellion against the King and in a fit of pique the Earl ejected the Durham monks and handed over the Priory to another Benedictine convent, St. Albans, in Hertfordshire.

It would seem that the monks who "misbehaved" in St. Albans were exiled to Tynemouth to help them see the error of their ways. One such luckless individual penned the following heartbreaking missive back to his colleagues.

"Our house is confined to the high rock and is surrounded by sea on every side. Day and night the waves break and roar and undermine the cliffs. Thick sea frets roll in, wrapping everything in gloom. Dim eyes, hoarse voice, sore throats are a consequence. Spring and summer never come here"...

If ever there was a strong incentive for the monks of St. Albans to behave, surely this must have been it.

In 1536 the agents of Henry V visited the Priory, then occupied by a Prior and fifteen monks. A number of the monks were criticized for being "immoral" and when the Priory was surrendered in 1539, the Prior and remaining monks were handsomely pensioned off. From this time the Priory and Castle functioned as one, in order to guard the mouth of the Tyne.

Time passed and those in authority found the cost of maintaining such a defence prohibitive and the buildings gradually fell into disrepair. In 1681 the defence of the Tyne was transferred to Clifford's Fort at North Shields.

R.W. Thornton 2000

Tyne Harbour

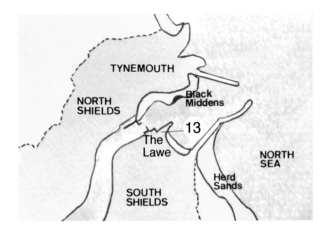

The Wouldhave Memorial

Over many centuries entering the River Tyne has been extremely hazardous. Vessels navigating the river face not only the notorious Black Middens rocks at the foot of Tynemouth cliffs, but also the equally dangerous Herd Sands across the other side of the harbour. Frequent storms sweeping in from the open sea, coupled with the shallow water at the bar could at times compound the problems of seafarers.

An indication of how shallow the water could be may be gleaned from the fact that in 1843, Robert Young, a Tyne pilot, waded across the bar from the Middens to the Herd Sands. Such conditions were responsible for numerous shipwrecks and the loss of countless lives. It is sad to learn that such tragic events often attracted huge crowds of onlookers on both shores; eager to witness but unable to help as luckless sailors perished in the cold waters.

In 1789 the, "Adventure" of Newcastle was wrecked on the bar, the entire crew perished. This tragedy galvanized the good people of Tynemouth into action, leading to the formation of a committee with the brief to design and build a lifeboat. Henry Greathead and William Wouldhave submitted designs. Eventually a model submitted by Greathead, albeit incorporating a number of aspects of Wouldhave's design, was accepted.

This first lifeboat, aptly named the, "Original" was launched in 1790 and in June of that year was instrumental in saving lives from a vessel grounded on the Middens. The "Original" continued to save innumerable lives over the next forty years. The Wouldhave Lifeboat Memorial is depicted above.

In 1854 work began on the construction of two piers to act as breakwaters. This immense task which was not completed until 1909 due to a series of setbacks, the most serious of which occurred in 1898, when the North Pier was breached during a storm and severely damaged due to a weakness in construction. This pier was originally designed as a curve to "dampen" the wave action, but on resumption was completed in a straight line.

The South Pier is a mile long and the North just over half a mile, with little more than a quarter mile separating the two lighthouses. After their completion the Tyne become a great deal safer.

1869 saw the formation of a Volunteer Life Brigade, the first in the country, based at Tynemouth. Their headquarters still stand on the cliff top below Collingwood's Monument, overlooking the mouth of the river.

R.W. THORNTON 2000

South Shields Waterfront

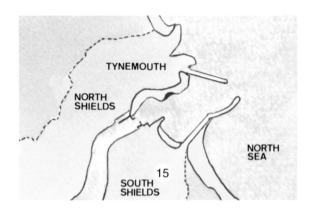

The Old Town Hall and Market

In AD 80, the Romans under the command of Agricola, built a substantial fortress, Arbeia, on the Lawe Top overlooking the mouth of the Tyne. It was a superb site developing into a strong military base combined with a commercial trading centre. Corn, cattle, wool and probably lead and iron could be exported readily by sea in direct exchange for goods from the continent, whilst supplies for the upkeep of Hadrian's Wall could be shipped up the Tyne as far as Corstopitum. This was the beginning of a major seaport.

Like her cross-river neighbour, South Shields suffered during the Middle Ages at the hands of the Newcastle monopolists who did all in their power, by fair means or otherwise, to stifle trading and industrial initiatives by what they regarded as the "river mouth upstarts." Despite this the town made significant progress and continued to expand.

In earlier times the staple trade had been the production of salt for fish preservation, during the mid sixteenth century the pall of smoke from the saltpans could be seen from the distant Cheviot Hills. By the end of the century South Shields was gaining significance as a seaport and shipbuilding began to overtake salt making. Industrial output was further increased by the manufacture of glass and chemicals. Robert Wallis established the first local shipyard in 1720, and the world's first iron-hulled vessel was built by Thomas Marshall in 1847. This was the "Conside", a screw steamer of two hundred and fifty nine tonnes, which marked a significant turning point in modern shipbuilding

As always, expanding industrial activity brought increasing social problems. Long, narrow, crooked streets ran along the riverfront from the Lawe to Jarrow Slake. This was an extremely busy and somewhat notorious thoroughfare, consisting of shops, taverns – open all hours to cater for the tides, brothels and warehouses. Housing was poor and highly overcrowded with little or no sanitation. In 1884 over one hundred residents died during a cholera epidemic. Attempts to cope were pitiful, mainly consisting of burning tar barrels in the streets and the sale of "cholera bottles" by unscrupulous apothecaries.

The Mill Dam, which used to be a tributary before infilling prior to use as part of the quayside, acted as a demarcation line. Those living to the east were known as "Fishers" (fishermen) and those to the west as "Panners" (salt makers). History suggests a long-running, alcohol-fuelled rivalry.

During its development South Shields recorded many significant milestones. The formation of the Seamen's Trade Union, the first registered steamboat passenger service and the creation of the Workingmen's Club movement as well as the founding of the world famous Marine College by Dr. Thomas Winterbottom. At one time the country's largest glass works was based here and the town still boasts the country's oldest provincial newspaper, the Shields Gazette which is still in print.

Today most of the heavy industry has disappeared and South Shields has changed from an industrial port to a seaside resort offering clean beaches, cliff-top walks, a bustling promenade, a shopping centre and excellent parks. Fittingly, the Roman fort, Arbeia, has been restored and is one or the town's main attractions.

R. W. Thornton 2000

North Shields Waterfront

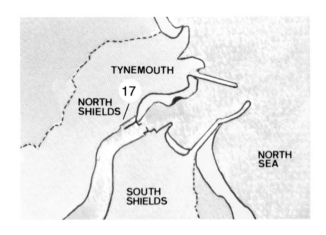

The Collingwood Memorial

In 1225, with support from a charter granted by Richard I, the Prior of Tynemouth, Brother Germanus attempted to establish a fishing port in order to provide fish as an inexpensive source of food for the resident monks. To this end twenty-seven crude huts or "shiels" (hence Shields) were built on a narrow strip of sand along the riverside west of the Priory. Each shiel had a wooden quay for mooring vessels and by the end of the thirteenth century over a hundred such buildings existed. The fishing trade had expanded significantly and was now augmented by a brisk trade in salt, coal, hides, wool and even imported wines.

The Mayor and Aldermen of Newcastle became increasingly infuriated by such progress. They considered it an illicit activity as they regarded all river trade and its subsequent revenue as entirely

their own. They were of the opinion that North Shields was "A town where no town ought to be." They mounted frequent raids on the settlement, causing widespread damage and personal injury. The Prior and his followers stubbornly held out. Repeated appeals to Parliament by the Newcastle monopolists were eventually rewarded when Edward I ordered the Prior to dismantle the quays on the grounds that they encroached upon the river and impeded navigation. It was not until 1390 that the settlement was re-established as a fishing and supplies port.

Riverside development eventually ran out of room for expansion. The huts were overcrowded with little or no sanitation; pigs roamed freely about the streets and plagues were frequent. In addition the dwellings were cheek to cheek with

dens of infamy, sailor's lodgings, ship's chandlers, roperies, salt pans and pubs – no fewer than fifty in a quarter-mile stretch. The area became notorious for its drinking dens and brothels around the aptly named, Low Street. According to a Royal Commission report at the time, it was the worst place in the Kingdom in this respect.

The only thoroughfare of consequence, Low Street was so called because of the town's position below sixty-foot cliffs. In 1760 residents were compelled to establish a new community on the cliff top – many moving en masse, so adding substance to the local aphorism, "Aal together, like the folks o' Shields" – and sensible thought was given to town planning. The two communities were linked by a series of connecting stairs (the bank was much too steep for a road) that survive today.

R.W. Thornton 2000

North Shields Fish Quay

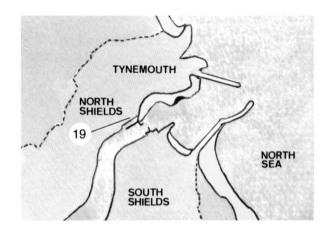

Mending the nets

In 1883 the protracted, bitter quarrel between the residents of the mouth of the Tyne and the merchants of Newcastle was largely resolved when North Shields was constituted as a fishing port. This required the enrolment of all local fishing vessels under the registration SN. NS would surely have been more sensible!

The Western fish quay built in 1850, was extended in 1887. Further shelter was provided when the Protection Quay was built parallel to the main fish quay and a covered fish market followed in 1897 which proved to be a significant development. Prior to this fish sold in the town was subject to tax; in protest the fishwives had sold their wares on the beach to the east of the Low Light tax-free. The new fish market however was free of tolls and quickly developed into a lively, thriving trade centre.

The famous "Fishwives" from nearby Cullercoats dressed in a traditional uniform of navy, serge dresses and tight-fitting bodices covered by a black shawl. They bought their quota of fish at the North Shields Market and, packed with ice into wicker baskets designed to be carried on the head or back, they toiled up the steep steps to Tynemouth Railway Station to catch the train to Newcastle.

As the fishing industry developed, the use of saltpans as a means of producing salt for fish curing grew dramatically. The Crown was not slow to recognize the profits from taxing salt. There are a number of local streets that include the name 'salter' dating back to the manufacture of salt.

In 1887 William Purdy, owner of the steam tug, "The Messenger", became frustrated at having to tow sailing vessels out to sea and back at the vagaries of the wind. He hit upon the idea of converting the tug into a steam-driven trawler – another first for the Tyne – and in 1879 covered himself in further glory and no doubt money too, by building the "Rose," the first ever stern–screw trawler. By 1907, North Shields was regarded as the premier white fish port in Britain.

In the late 1940's many a young lad would take a sack to the Fish Quay. He would be allowed to pick up the fish that slipped from the loading baskets or "crans" as they were being lifted ashore. Filling the sack with as much fish as he could carry and topped up with ice he would make his way home. Once there he would sell the catch around the doors for "sweetie money."

Despite the uncertainty surrounding the industry, North Shields remains an important fishing port.

18

Tyne Tugs

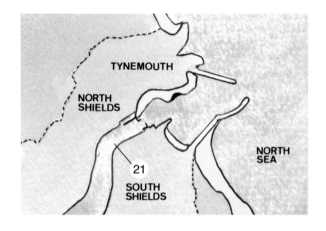

Paddle Tug

In 1814, a steam-driven paddle ship was built at Gateshead to operate as a passenger ferry between Newcastle and the river mouth. It was not a success and was sold to Mr. Price, an early entrepreneur who had the revolutionary idea of using the vessel to tow ships out to sea beyond the bar. Hitherto they had moved downriver from Newcastle entirely dependent on sail and prevailing wind conditions. With the aid of steam, the thirteen-mile journey took a fraction over two hours, an enormous time saving. This enabled the coal-laden colliers to substantially increase the number of sailings to the Port of London.

By 1818, tugboat towing, as it became known, was firmly established on the Tyne. Over the next few years the concept spread rapidly to the neighbouring ports and rivers. Fourteen tugs were soon operating on the the Tyne, over the next ten years the number increased to thirty; all wooden-hulled and driven by steam. Iron hulls were introduced in 1880 but it was to be a further sixty years before the wooden-hulled tugs finally disappeared. Towards the end of the nineteenth century screw-propelled tugs were also working the river and the end of the Second World War saw the introduction of the diesel engine. Far cheaper to run, but conversion was a slow process and steam-driven tugs continued to operate for another twenty-five years.

In addition to the basic functions of towing and docking, potentially good money could be earned from salvage. By the second half of the twentieth century local tugs would leave the comparative safety of the river and sail the coast often in appalling weather, soliciting vessels destined for northeast ports. Haggling was common until a tow charge was agreed.

By this time the Tyne tugs had a crew of six. Skipper, chief engineer, mate, two deckhands and the "boy". The boy was a veritable dogsbody who not only had to cook and keep the bilges clear of water - one presumes he washed his hands - but also had to scull the small foy boat ashore to fetch beer, place bets, pick up crew members and collect the weekly wages. Before the advent of mobile phones, crewmembers were alerted to imminent tows by the "yellow peril," a yellow form with sailing details that was delivered by taxi. Stories are told of names being flashed up on cinema screens and crewmembers making a swift exit, leaving behind many an irate young lady.

Cory Tugs bought out Tyne and Wear Tugs in 1995 and they, in turn, were taken over by a Dutch firm, Wijsmuller in 2000. Leaving only three tugs left to work the entire length of the Tyne.

R.W. THORNTON 2000

Early Tyne Ferries

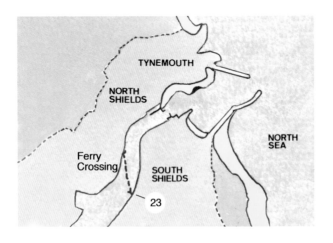

The Northumbrian

As early as 1377 ferry services were operating between North and South Shields. The ferries were little more than small rowing or sculling boats, which were often overloaded leading to many tragedies. One recorded incident in 1760 is of a boat carrying twelve people which overturned with the loss of ten lives.

A few decades later in 1798 an engineer named Dodd proposed a revolutionary method of river crossing. He set out a scheme for a circular tunnel, fourteen feet in diameter to be buried under the river, the project never came to fruition.

In the early nineteenth century Royal Assent was given to establish a ferry crossing and the North East Ferry Co. was created. The company operated three vessels; the Baron Newcastle, the Durham and the Northumberland. Some years later a rival company, the Tyne Direct Ferry set up in competition. They ran a single passenger-only ferry known locally as the Halfpenny Dodger that ran a more direct route between Comical Corner, South Shields and the New Quay, North Shields. It was a popular service as it was quicker and cheaper than the alternative company.

In 1863 the Tyne Improvement Commission took over the two ferry companies as part of their river improvement scheme. Over the next sixty years they commissioned thirteen ferries, the last vessel was the Northumbrian which is illustrated. The tunnel project was revived, a proposal was made for a 'tube railway' with lifts at either end to convey passengers to and from ground level stations. The idea was under consideration for twenty years before being abandoned.

Throughout the 1950's and 1960s three ferries; the South Shields, the Tynemouth and the Northumbrian provided particularly sterling service, carrying four hundred thousand vehicles and countless foot passengers each year. Later the service was taken over by the Tyne and Wear Passenger Transport Executive, who built the Freda Cunningham and the Shieldsman. They had a radically new design, were diesel powered and only carried foot passengers, ending the era of vehicle crossing between the two towns.

The poor old Northumbrian suffered the indignity of being converted to a floating restaurant moored at Gateshead, before finally closing in 1976.

South Shields Ferry Landing

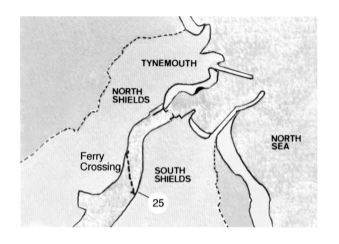

The Shieldsman

Prior to 1967 the ferry service between North and South Shields carried both vehicles and foot passengers. The opening of the Tyne Tunnel from Wallsend to Jarrow created a dramatic decline in the number of vehicles carried by ferry.

In 1972 two new ferries were built, both carrying foot passengers only but each of a very different design. The "Freda Cunningham" cost £304,000 but unfortunately quickly gained a dreadful reputation. One local dignitary proclaimed, "Her record is a public disgrace. She cannot be relied upon. She is extremely noisy. Her decks leak." Elsewhere she was labelled, "A stop-go problem ship" and "An overgrown tug" However her counterpart, the "Shieldsman" could do little wrong. She enjoyed a revolutionary double-ended design that allowed her to dock and sail without the need to turn, thus saving valuable time in addition to fuel and engine wear.

In 1978 a ferry sank in the middle of the night due to the ballast tanks, which supported the structure, flooding. Both the above ferries, moored to the landing at the time, were cast adrift but fortunately the night watchman's frantic calls for help were picked up on radio by a tug conveniently moored across the river. The ferries were saved without any real damage being done.

The ferry landing was damaged again in 1987 when, during gale force winds a large vessel, the "Rora Head", broke free of its moorings and was swept downriver, ramming the landing during its progress.

Swan Hunter landed a much needed £1.4 million contract to build a new ferry, "The Pride of the Tyne" in 1992. This was to replace the disgraced twenty-year old "Freda Cunningham" and to run in tandem with the "Shieldsman." The new design was on the same lines as the Shieldsman but with minor modifications. She was the smallest ship ever to be built by the yard and was not launched in the conventional manner but lowered into the water by crane. Sadly she was also the last vessel to be built by the yard.

Shortly afterwards the "Freda Cunningham" suffered the final indignity of being taken out of service and sold off as scrap. The ill-fated ferry landing was declared a danger to the public, after inspection by engineers revealed that the entire structure needed to be replaced. Admiral Sir Nigel Essenhigh opened the new landing, a strikingly modern design by Bill Ainsworth.

R.W. Thornton 2000

Readheads Shipyard

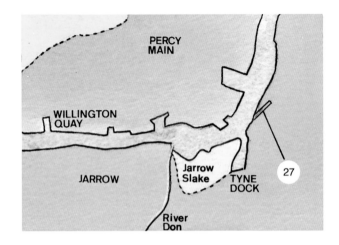

Floating Repairs

The founder, John Readhead, started his working life as a millwright on the north bank of the river. At the age of thirty-two he crossed the Tyne to train as a shipwright. His enthusiasm and ability swiftly raised him to the position of yard manager. After fifteen years he entered into partnership with J. Softley and they commenced shipbuilding from premises at the Lawe, near Pilot Street.

The partnership was dissolved in 1872 and Readhead formed his own company. During the next sixteen years, one hundred vessels were built and the yard established a reputation for quality and reliability. As the business prospered the yard expanded by purchasing the adjacent west docks.

In addition to shipbuilding and engine fitting, the river frontage was adapted to allow floating ship repairs to take place. The decision to incorporate ship repairs was farsighted as later events were to prove.

It is fascinating to learn that in these times the local pub, the "Cookson Arms," opened its doors at six in the morning and literally covered the bar with tots of rum for thirsty customers to sup up before starting the day's work. One wonders how many accidents and fatalities occurred as a result of the alcohol-affected start to the working day.

The Admiralty took control of Readheads during the First World War and the following years became a period of frenzied activity. The repair section was in great demand due to mine and torpedo damage. Fortunes changed however, as in 1931 the Tyneside area was enveloped by the Great Depression. At Readheads only the apprentices and their supervisors were kept on; virtually the whole of the workforce was laid off for five years. Only one vessel was built during this period and the repair section again proved to be a lifeline.

Business slowly improved, then in 1939 war clouds gathered again. As had happened twenty-five years earlier, production was back to virtually full strength as demand for shipping dramatically increased to cope with the Second World War.

In 1968 Readheads was taken over by Swan Hunter Shipbuilders Ltd. The last ship to be built in the Shields yard was the coaster, " Singularity," launched in 1977 prior to nationalization. The yard concentrated on repair work until closed by British Shipbuilders in 1982. It was later leased back to a company formed by Readhead's workforce, who raised the sum of £110,000 by pooling their redundancy money. Sadly, after just eighteen months, financial difficulties brought about liquidation; a bitter pill to swallow for such a loyal and dedicated group of employees.

R.W. THORNTON 2000

Jarrow - St. Bede

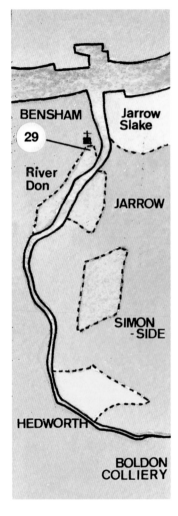

The River Don

Jarrow is possibly best known because of "local lad" the Venerable Bede, who lived most of his life and died in Jarrow Monastery. Benedict Biscop, Abbot of Wearmouth, founded the Monastery in 681. Bede entered the establishment from the nearby hamlet of Monkton at the age of seven to be educated. He went on to produce many great works. It is said that he was still writing, or more likely dictating, on his deathbed in the year 735. Probably his greatest work was the, "History of the English Church and People", in which he set out the date of Christ's birth and thus created the form of dating – Anno Domini – in the year of Our Lord.

Other works served to underline the range and depth of his knowledge and were acclaimed all over Europe. On his death he was buried in the north side of the monastery church; his remains were later taken to Durham Cathedral to lie alongside those of his great contemporary, St. Cuthbert.

A notable feature of the area is Jarrow Slake, pronounced locally as Slack. This is a remarkable tidal mudflat three miles from the river mouth. Before the river was widened and deepened it served as a much needed flood relief when the Tyne was in full spate. The Slake, fully submerged at high water, was used for many years as a timber-seasoning pond. It was also the scene of the last public gibbeting in the country. In 1832, William Jobling was hanged for murder. After the execution his body was coated with pitch and hung from the gibbet for three weeks under military guard as a public warning. The body then mysteriously disappeared, probably buried secretly by family and friends. Eventually evidence came to light that proved that poor Jobling had been innocent of the crime.

Today much of the Slake has been reclaimed for industrial use. Jarrow, along with its neighbours, benefited from the boom in shipbuilding and associated industries in the years prior to 1914 but depression in the early thirties caused industry to collapse. One of the worst blows was the liquidation of Palmers Shipbuilding and Iron Company. Massive unemployment and general misery led to the famous Jarrow March of 1936. This won widespread public sympathy but fell on deaf ears in Whitehall.

Jarrow has recovered somewhat since, but bitter memories of the times have been dramatically depicted in the novels of locally-born Catherine Cookson. She once said: "I couldn't write with any strength about any other place."

R.W. Thornton 2000

Swan Hunter

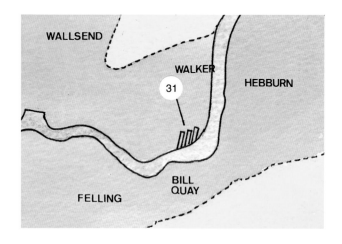

Wallsend Yard

In 1873 Charles Mitchell started shipbuilding at Wallsend and employed his brother in law, Charles Sheriton Swan as yard manager. The firm was registered as C. S. Swan & Co. Unfortunately the industrious Swan was killed when he fell overboard from a Channel ferry in 1879. Subsequently George Barton Hunter, a Sunderland shipbuilder entered into partnership with Swan's widow and the firm was renamed, C. S. Swan & Hunter, becoming a limited company in 1895.

Eight years later the maritime world was in a state of great excitement when a prestigious contract to build a Cunard Queen, the R M S Mauretania was announced. At the time it was undoubtedly the biggest prize any yard could have hoped for. Competition for the order was extremely fierce.

Efforts to secure it led Swans to join forces with a neighbouring firm, John Wigham Richardson, from the Neptune yard at Wallsend. Their joint bid was successful, paving the way for permanent amalgamation with a reputation throughout the world for marine craftsmanship and reliability second to none. The Wallsend yard established itself as the main structural builder, while the Neptune yard concentrated more on the construction of ship's engines.

In 1906 and again in 1912, the Company held the world record for the gross tonnage of shipping constructed. Altogether, during a period of one hundred and twenty years, more than sixteen hundred vessels were built. They included passenger and cargo liners, ferries, oil tankers, icebreakers, frigates, submarines and aircraft

carriers. No doubt they would have made a first class job of Noah's Ark had they been operating at the time.

1993 saw the unbelievable event. The renowned Tyne shipbuilders called in the receivers after failing to win a vital order for the helicopter carrier, "H M S Ocean." On the third of November 1994 the last vessel, the frigate "H M S Richmond" left the Wallsend yard for delivery to the Royal Navy. It was an extremely moving occasion with many tears being shed. The collapse created great bitterness, many blaming the Government for lack of support. The Neptune yard was eventually sold for ship repair purposes. This however was not the end. The Dutch-owned T H C Group bought the Wallsend yard for £5 million in June 1995.

Tyneside Shipbuilding

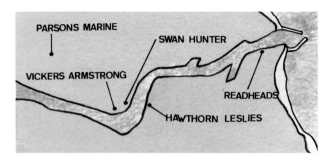

Mauretania on trials

The Mauretania

The Mauretania was built by Swan Hunter at their Wallsend yard and was launched by the Dowager Duchess of Roxburgh. At thirty two thousand tonnes, Swans had to make special arrangements for her construction. Ground conditions needed to be strengthened; this was achieved by driving over fifteen hundred wooden pilings. In addition a huge weatherproof shed was needed to protect the hull and superstructure during building.

Newly-developed Parsons' steam turbine engines were installed which would allow her to cruise at twenty-seven knots. This enabled her to capture the Blue Riband for the fastest Atlantic crossing in 1907 and hold it for twenty-two years. The ornate, luxurious accommodation catered for two and a half thousand passengers plus a crew of eight hundred. She quickly earned the title of "The Floating Palace." All in all it took just twenty-nine months from signing the contract to delivery and can justifiably be regarded as one of the greatest achievements in British shipbuilding.

The Turbinia

In 1897 Charles Parsons made a presentation to the world's leading navies gathered at the Spithead Review, when he audaciously unleashed his craft, The Turbinia, on an unsuspecting world. The Turbinia astounded the military by weaving in and out of the warships at the unheard of speed of thirty-four knots, leaving the crews open-mouthed in disbelief. The Royal Navy was not a little displeased at this unheralded upstaging, however Parsons had made his point in this most dramatic way and from then on the world queued at his door to obtain the revolutionary steam turbine engine.

H.M.S. Kelly

Hawthorn Leslie won a contract in 1936 to build two destroyers at their Hebburn yard; one of them was the Kelly. Commissioned in 1939, her strengthened hull, sleek design, newly-laid-out engine room and the different distribution of her armament singled the Kelly out as being radically different from her predecessors. She also had the distinction of Lord Louis Mountbatten as commander.

Her war career quickly became legendary and was immortalized in the film, "In Which We Serve."

She was frequently attacked, suffering severe damage and loss of life but returned to action again and again and became a symbol of defiance, inspiring the nation when the war was going badly. Eventually she was bombed and sunk in May 1941, just twenty months after being launched. To this day her name elicits a warm response with the people of Tyneside.

Esso Northumbria

In 1970 thousands of Tynesiders thronged the banks of the river to watch this huge vessel of one hundred and twenty six thousand tonnes glide out to sea. She was the first of the supertankers to be built by Swan Hunter and, at the time, was the largest vessel ever to be built on the river. Her awesome size caused a "buzz" and rekindled interest in the long and distinguished history of Tyneside shipbuilding following years of relatively uneventful production.

Unfortunately oil demand slumped dramatically as worldwide recession bit deeply and many of these vessels were laid up. Even worse: maintenance costs during their enforced idleness were extremely high and led to a number of these huge vessels being sold for scrap.

P.W. Thornton 2000

St Peter's Basin

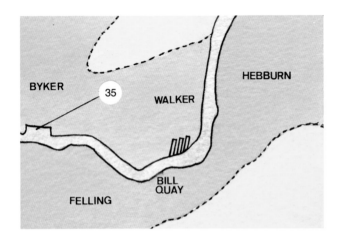

The Marina

St. Peter's is now the location of houses, flats, offices, a pub, a modern marina and a small number of related shops. It was an area where people who lived in urban poverty worked; it is now an area where the affluent can work, rest and play.

The site was once the location of the St. Peter's Works of R & W. Hawthorn which became Hawthorn Leslie in 1886, a firm renowned throughout the world for the manufacture of marine engines. In the 1880s machinery was transferred from Hawthorn's Forth Bank Works to enable the factory to keep up with demand. The Newcastle and Riverside branch line of the North East Railway passed through the site and St. Peter's had a station and goods yard. Maps dating from the end of the nineteenth century and aerial photographs from the 1980s clearly show that St. Peter's Basin was dominated by heavy industry. Further along the Tyne towards the Ouseburn was the St. Lawrence Foreign Cattle Sanatorium, which was developed in the mid-1870s to quarantine livestock imported from Denmark and elsewhere within Europe.

Prior to redevelopment St Peter's Basin could only be described as an area of urban industrial blight. In the 1980s the site was cleared of industrial remains and the marina was constructed. Opened in 1990, it has the boast of being the most sheltered marina in the country and can accommodate craft up to eighty feet in length with a maximum draught of ten feet.

A North Sea storm in 1992 brought a group of German yachts into the marina. Some of them ended up staying a year and St. Peter's Marina is now well known to members of the German yachting community. The marina is also a popular destination for people from the Netherlands and Scandinavia. The Tyne Bridge Winter Series of races held every other Sunday ensures that the marina is busy all year round.

The Ouseburn

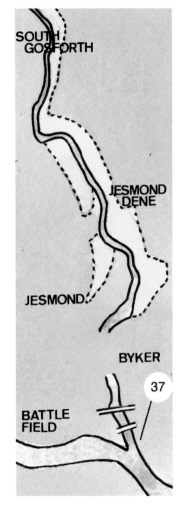

The Gut

The Ouseburn is a small but historically important tributary of the Tyne, which enters the main river to the east of Newcastle through a compact valley. In the past the area was largely agricultural, which suggests the name may be a corruption of "Ewesburn."

The Ouseburn is a classic case of being in the right place at the right time. The junction with the Tyne formed a wide enough area for most vessels to be able to turn and manoeuvre, a distinct advantage as the river in the nineteenth century was barely navigable due to lack of dredging and indiscriminate dumping of ballast. The Ouseburn was deep enough to be negotiated by keel boats as far up as the Byker Bridge thus ensuring movement of supplies. Furthermore its close proximity to the sea, plentiful supply of coal and fast-flowing water to drive mills ensured that the area became highly industrialized.

The upper reaches of the Ouseburn managed to retain some rural charm but the lower stretches quickly became filled up with a range of industrial works leading to a huge increase in population. Living conditions were appalling, with many families surviving in one room sharing primitive toilet facilities. The Ouseburn then, was regarded as an open sewer and the City Medical Officer of Health attacked the widespread use of the, "privy Pail" system. This was basically a bucket shared by up to four families and emptied by the Council three times a week. Such dreadful conditions led to an inevitable outbreak of typhoid fever from which twenty-four died. To add to the problems the various factories were belching out a noxious mix of chemical fumes and waste both day and night. It comes as no surprise that the infant mortality rate was almost twenty per cent.

Attempts were made to improve conditions and a notable step forward was the building of the Ouseburn school by the Newcastle architect F.W. Rich in 1893. Its unusual pagoda-like twin towers with their distinctive oriental look, (seen in the main painting) were part of the ventilation system, and have become a well-known landmark.

As the twentieth century progressed the rapid developments of roads, railways and bridges along both banks of the Tyne led to improved access throughout the area and industry gradually moved away and the Ouseburn began to decline.

In the late 1960s the City Council approved the "Ouseburn Project", which was a scheme to develop the run-down valley from the Tyne banks to Gosforth as a single tourist area. A green corridor to encourage wildlife has since been created, plus parks, streams and open spaces. The project is now well established, with many buildings being renovated and a museum set up to preserve the industrial heritage of the area.

R.W. Thornton 2000

Newcastle – Old Bridges

Pons Aelius

Roman Bridge

The Emperor Hadrian built the very first bridge over the Tyne circa AD 122 prior to building the famous frontier wall. The crossing was in alignment with the present Swing Bridge and designed to carry the road from the existing fort at Concangis (Chester-le-Street) to a fort yet to be built at Newcastle.

Indications are that the bridge was a substantial structure. It is believed to have been built of timber supported by masonry piers with cutwaters both up and down stream and stone abutments on each bank. Two stone altars and an inscription, (dredged from the river many years later), formed a small archway at the centre of the bridge.

The crossing was named Pons Aelius in honour of the Emperor's family name. The family crest depicted a goat's head and a stone, bearing just such a carving was apparently fixed to the southern end of the bridge, hence the possible corruption, Gateshead. Records of crossings go back to 1248 when the bridge was destroyed by fire.

Medieval Bridge

The Medieval Bridge was built circa 1250, aligned along and using the remains of the Roman Bridge. The bridge was an important part of Newcastle's defences, guarding the southern approaches not only from rebellious armies but also from plague-ridden travellers - both capable of great destruction. For this reason formidable guard towers were built and continually manned at both ends of the bridge. The bridge must have been the hub of the town, as it was crowded with shops and houses, and had turreted towers and a chapel. It was one of the busiest areas in Newcastle.

The Aldermen of Newcastle and the Bishops of Durham demonstrated rare cooperation while the bridge was being built, but this was not to last. Lengthy and often bitter disputes ensued over the years as to who would have control over the bridge. In 1417 it was decreed that the Prince Bishops of Durham be given control over a third of the bridge on the Gateshead side and a blue stone was inset to mark the official boundary. This was known as "St. Cuthbert's Stone" and is now in the Keep at the Newcastle Museum.

Constant repairs were required and raising funds proved to be no easy task. It is mentioned that the Durham clerics resorted to the dubious practice of selling "remissions of time to be spent in purgatory" in exchange for money, materials or labour – thus catering for all classes of citizen. In 1771 the bridge was virtually destroyed by the Great Flood with the loss of six lives. If the disaster had occurred during daytime, the loss of life could have been catastrophic.

Georgian Tyne Bridge

This handsome stone bridge was also built on the alignment of both the Roman and Medieval Bridges and replaced the latter. With its many arches the Georgian Tyne Bridge was not without a certain grace and elegance. Foundation stones were laid at Gateshead in 1774 and Newcastle in 1775.

The construction of the bridge was under the watchful eye of Mr. J. Mylne until the official opening in 1781. It is interesting to learn that the blue boundary stone, recovered during the demolition of the remains of the Medieval Bridge, was reset into the new bridge; old habits die hard! The bridge was initially tolled to help cover the high construction costs and it was not until 1818 that the toll was withdrawn.

The design of the bridge, although aesthetically pleasing, had serious flaws. Its broad piers and abutments occupied no less than one third of the total waterway causing serious water displacement. In effect it acted as a weir and, at times made navigation very difficult. More importantly it made up river dredging impracticable, a major obstacle to future development. In 1851 it was recommended that it be replaced by a new 'opening' bridge.

R. W. Thornton 2000

Millennium Bridge

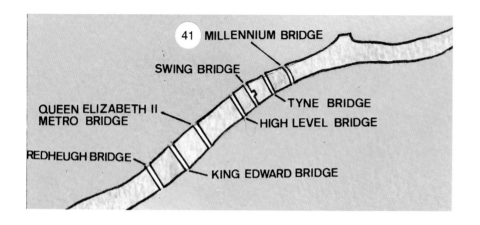

The Baltic Arts Centre

In 1996, Gateshead Council took the bold decision to enter the race for Millennium Funding and announced a design competition for a new opening bridge to link Gateshead with Newcastle. The brief was to create an attractive structure that would promote the river as a Tyneside asset instead of a barrier between the two long-standing communities. It was also to enhance the existing views.

One hundred and fifty entries worldwide were received from architect and engineering design teams, from which a short list of six designs was compiled. The panel of judges unanimously declared the design by Gifford and Partners (engineers) and Wilkinson Eyre (architects) to be the winner. Funding was sought from the Millennium Commission and in 1997 a grant of £9.2 million was awarded, amounting to roughly half the building costs of the new bridge.

The unique tilting design is yet another world first for Tyneside. The movement of the bridge can be compared to the opening and closing of a huge eyelid, hence the "Blinking Eye". As always, river navigation played a significant role in the design. The bridge provides a navigational channel of thirty metres, equal to the Swing Bridge, and a headroom clearance, when open, of twenty-five metres, equal to the Tyne Bridge. A series of steel fender piles were placed in the river to mark the navigation path and to prevent the bridge supports from being damaged by collision. These have attracted wide criticism as being both unnecessary and detracting from the stunning design of the bridge.

The arch and deck were fabricated by Watson Steel based in Bolton, while the opening mechanism was manufactured in Sheffield. The frame was built at the Amec Yard in Wallsend. In October 2000, one of the world's largest floating cranes,

Asian Hercules II, caused a stir of excitement when it arrived to lift the bridge into position. Three days of guaranteed good weather were essential before the journey up river could take place. Disappointingly, bad weather caused delays and it was not until the twentieth of November that the great day arrived and the bridge was transported majestically up river and lowered into place with complete precision. Nothing had ever been seen like this before and local interest was enormous. Many thousands gathered to witness the historical moment while millions followed the event on worldwide television.

The new bridge became a world-famous landmark overnight and more than holds its own in what must be regarded as the finest "collection" of historic bridges anywhere in the world.

R.W. THORNTON 2002

Tyne Bridge

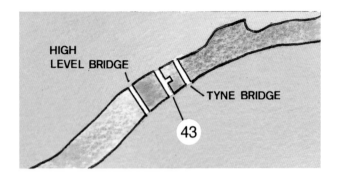

The Swing Bridge

By the end of the nineteenth century, clearly there was a need for another bridge to span the River Tyne. The High Level Bridge was chronically congested and the Swing Bridge's frequent openings compounded the traffic problem. In 1893 a committee was formed to discuss future strategy. Once again many years of wrangling passed until it became glaringly obvious that a new bridge was needed and soon! Finally the Gateshead and Newcastle Councils agreed on the need for urgent action and an Act of Parliament was obtained in 1924 to build a new bridge.

Before work could begin various objections had to be overcome. The Tyne Improvement Commission stipulated clearance above river level must be eighty-five feet, no piers were to be placed in the river and shipping must not be obstructed during the course of building. The upper arches were built out over the river from each bank simultaneously and a story of the time tells of the indignation of the Gateshead costermongers who viewed the emerging arch with dismay. A letter of protest was sent to the authorities complaining that it would be impossible for their horses and carts to negotiate such a steep incline!

In October 1928 King George V, accompanied by Queen Mary opened the Tyne Bridge, which at the time was the largest single-span bridge in the country. Strangely enough its handsome towers have little structural value, and apparently were designed as five storey warehouses but the floors were never installed. However lifts were in place to allow access to the quaysides for both passengers and goods. Talk of converting the towers to luxury flats as part of the on-going modern regeneration programme has yet to come to fruition.

The bridge presents a dramatic landmark that evokes the spirit of Tyneside the world over and continues to bring a warm glow of homecoming to returning Geordies.

Tyne Bridges

Mylne's Georgian Tyne Bridge, built in 1781 to replace the Medieval Bridge swept away ten years earlier in the Great Flood, proved to be very unpopular. The low stone arches, while pleasing to look at prevented all but the smallest boats from passing up river. This hindered industrial development along the river banks west of Newcastle.

The Georgian Tyne Bridge

The replacement led to bitter debate relating to location, height, width and design. There was probably more anguish displayed over this project than for any previous river crossing and hitherto there had been a great deal! Eventually the Tyne Improvement Commission obtained permission to build a revolutionary opening swing bridge on the same site as the Georgian road bridge.

By 1867 the bickering had diminished and Mylne's bridge began to be dismantled. One individual who benefited in particular was William Armstrong. The Newcastle-born engineering genius had created an industrial power base until now confined up river at Elswick. This development was instrumental in allowing massive expansion of his engineering empire; in fact the hydraulically-driven, new replacement bridge was designed and built at his Elswick works. When the bridge was opened it was the largest hydraulic bridge in the world. It was also fitting that the first vessel to pass through was the "Europa," collecting guns from Armstrong's works to take to the Italian Navy.

Originally the bridge was steam-powered and used over a ton of coal per week. In 1959 it was converted to an electrically-driven power system. In early days ships had to give four hours' notice of arrival and the bridge could only remain open for fifteen minutes at a time. Ten minutes before opening a steam whistle blew to alert road traffic with a continuous bell sounding as a final warning.

Initially the demand on the bridge by river traffic was disappointingly light and the repayment of building costs by the toll charged looked far from promising. It was not until 1893 that the establishment of the coal staithes above Newcastle brought a dramatic increase in river traffic and a financial upturn. The bridge opened on average thirty times per day, the peak year being 1924, when six thousand vessels passed through. Altogether nearly half a million ships have made this passage to the upper reaches of the Tyne since 1876.

The original machinery is still in full working order and the bridge is opened on special occasions; it is now a listed structure.

High Level Bridge

As long ago as 1772 there were proposals for a bridge at high level to allow a "noble entrance" across the Tyne into Newcastle. This was to avoid the steep climb up and down the river bank and the noise, smell and general ugliness of the slums crowding the riverside. First time round the project was too far ahead of its time and was shelved.

The coming of the railways galvanized action. At the time the rail line stopped at Gateshead and passengers from Newcastle had to be ferried across the river and then climb a steep flight of steps up to Redheugh Railway Station. An intolerable state of affairs according to Mr. George Hudson, dubbed the "Railway King" who instigated a direct rail link between London and Edinburgh and in doing so heralded the construction of the High Level Bridge.

The bridge, designed by Robert Stephenson, son of George, is a unique double-decked structure; carrying three rail tracks on the upper deck with a roadway beneath. Apparently a Mr. William Martin had submitted a strikingly similar plan a year previously and claimed his idea had been "stolen." The structure was the first ever dual deck road/rail bridge in the world with around five thousand tons of local wrought iron and cast iron being used in its construction.

The rail deck runs one hundred and twelve feet above the high water mark and piling had to be driven deep into the riverbed to support the massive stone piers. Nasmyth's newly invented steam-hammer "Titanic" was used to drive home the wooden piles. The rapid strokes produced so much frictional heat that the piles often burst into flames.

Queen Victoria declared the bridge open in September 1849. It seems that after the completion of the opening ceremony, a Mr. Williamson jumped from the parapet into the river after being bet a quart of beer. He accepted the bet, jumped and survived to eventually claim his drink. One wonders how much he had already had!

R.W. Thornton 2000

Queen Elizabeth II Metro Bridge

The Metro railway was designed to become Britain's first, fully-integrated transport system. In order to achieve this yet another bridge to cross the Tyne was required. This would be the new Metro line to Gateshead and then eastwards along the river bank to the terminus at South Shields.

The Queen Elizabeth Bridge is sited between the High Level and King Edward Bridges and had to comply with a number of stringent conditions. Regulations were drawn up by the various authorities empowered to oversee the project and stipulated that; the construction must not overshadow neighbouring bridges, its appearance must have the approval of the local art and environmental bodies, it must be built at minimum cost and no piers were to be placed in the river to impede navigation.

Such formidable parameters did not deter the designers who created a clear, single-span twin track, supported by concrete piers. The Queen, accompanied by the Duke of Edinburgh, opened the bridge in 1981.

The Queen Elizabeth II Metro Bridge

King Edward Bridge

After fifty years of service the High Level Bridge was becoming critically overloaded due to the phenomenal growth of rail travel. There must have been some regret that the original proposal for a four-line track had been reduced to three to save costs. It was necessary to build a further rail link across the Tyne: the King Edward Bridge.

Originally the bridge was to consist of two lattice girder spans with a series of land approach arches, similar to the High Level. However when excavating began, old mine workings were revealed at either end of the bridge, causing many of the proposed arches to be abandoned. The bridge was eventually built with four massive steel lattice girders supported by three large concrete pillars with the emphasis being on no-nonsense efficiency rather than elegance. King Edward VII opened the bridge in July 1906 and then went on to the R. V. I. to unveil a statue of his mother, Queen Victoria, whom he had accompanied fifty-one years earlier when she opened the High Level Bridge. The King Edward Bridge was the first rail bridge to carry four main tracks and at the time created a great deal of interest. Unfortunately this bridge is also showing its limitations, the gaps between the railway tracks are too narrow to allow the new generation of high speed trains to pass safely.

R.W. Thornton 2000

Redheugh Bridge

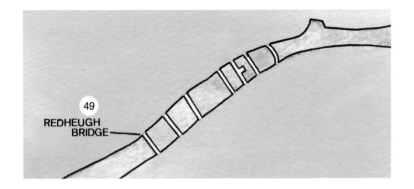

The Second Redheugh Bridge

In 1860, builder Richard Cail proposed a rail/road bridge at Redheugh on the Gateshead side of the river with the rail deck below the road level, the reverse of the High Level Bridge. North Eastern Rail showed little interest so Cail, with others, decided to press ahead with a road bridge only. 1866 saw the required Parliamentary permission obtained and the design of the bridge was entrusted to Sir Thomas Bouch, the same man who was later to design the infamous Tay Bridge, which collapsed with the loss of one hundred and seventy lives.

The Redheugh Bridge was a slender construction with a footpath either side. It was supported by three river piers thirty metres above river level. However construction was hindered by delays in the delivery of materials, due to poor access roads and the scarcity of skilled labour. In May 1871 the bridge opened and as early as 1885 serious structural faults began to emerge. The general opinion was that repairs would cost more than a new bridge.

Replacement commenced in 1897 with the new bridge being built around the old structure. Once again progress was hindered by delays in materials and an inadequate work force. By 1900 the main girders and spans were in place and, ingeniously, hydraulic jacks were used to inch along the newly built superstructure until it rested on the previously constructed piers. The remains of the old structure were then removed and the bridge was opened in August 1907.

The only road alternative at the time was the already overcrowded High Level Bridge. As a consequence the new bridge quickly enjoyed a high volume of traffic and the tolls charged brought in revenue. This fell away soon after, when tolls were scrapped on the High Level. By 1965 speed and weight restrictions of ten mph. and ten tons made the bridge virtually non-viable. Once again there was talk of a replacement being built to cope with the relentlessly-increasing flow of traffic.

The third Redheugh Bridge couldn't have been more different in appearance from its two predecessors. It is one of the finest examples of a modern medium-span design, built with pre-stressed concrete and carrying four lanes of traffic with a single footway. The two supporting concrete piers were fluted to create an impression of lightness and were designed to withstand the impact from a vessel of ten thousand tonnes travelling at a speed of five knots.

Opened by the Princess of Wales in 1984, its delicate, flowing lines form a striking contrast with the heavy, industrial construction of its nearby companions.

R.W. THORNTON 2000

Dunston Staithes

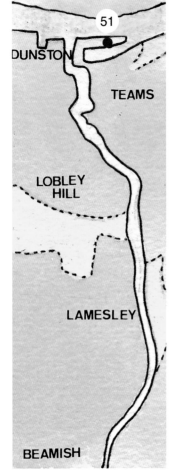

Dunston Staithes

As early as 1771, the Tyne keelmen staged a bitter and protracted strike protesting against proposals to build staithes near the river mouth. This would enable enable coal to be loaded directly into the holds of the waiting colliers by means of a chute or spout as opposed to the time-honoured tradition of loading by hand by the keelmen. They were successful and it was not until 1820 that the first direct-loading coal staithes gained a foothold on the lower reaches of the Tyne. The keelmen, not to be deterred, made numerous but largely unsuccessful assaults on the "accursed spouts." They argued that they were a navigational hazard and, more importantly, a threat to their livelihood.

Colliery owners upriver, enviously watched downriver developments as they were still forced to rely on the old system of keelboats to carry coal down to the waiting colliers where the cargo was laboriously transferred by hand. The problem was not solved until the newly formed Tyne Improvement Commission carried out extensive dredging works upriver. This was followed by the demolition of the low-arched Georgian Tyne Bridge in 1874 to make way for the Swing Bridge. For the first time large vessels, including colliers, could now venture up the river as far as Dunston and beyond. Colliery owners were delighted and pressed for rail links from their pits to the banks of the river, a privilege long enjoyed by their harbour counterparts. After some wrangling, the railway agreed to such a link from Anfield Plain via the Team Valley to Dunston where the staithes would be built.

The first stage of the staithes was completed in 1893. A second stage built into the riverbank to the south, forming a tidal basin, was opened in 1903.

The staithes stretched over five hundred and fifty yards and had three loading berths, each with two spouts. The lowest was twelve yards above high water and the highest over fourteen yards. The difference in heights allowed for loading whatever the state of the tide. The depth of water at low tide was a comfortable five and a half yards. On completion it was thought to be the largest wooden structure in the world.

The early years of the twentieth century saw the introduction of electrically driven conveyor belts that would carry the coal to the waiting spouts. The loading was overseen by shore-based workmen: "teamers" who supervised the actual loading via the spouts and "trimmers" who, using shovels, levelled the coal in the collier's holds to ensure stability, known as "knocking the tops off." At its peak in the 1920's one hundred and forty thousand tons of coal were shipped from the staithes per week. Dunston Staithes remained in use until 1983 and in 1986 became and scheduled Ancient Monument.

R.W. Thornton 2000

Derwenthaugh Staithes

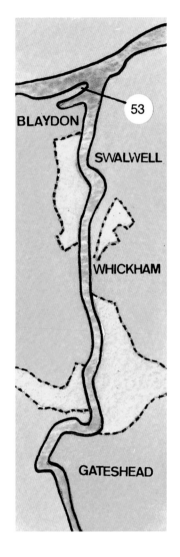

The Confluence

The River Derwent is the largest of the main Tyne tributaries. It rises on a moor near Allenheads and occasionally forms a natural border between Durham and Northumberland. After passing through Blanchland it is dammed to form the Derwent reservoir. When it reaches the Tyne, industry replaces rural tranquillity. Here was the location of early iron works, paper mills and brickworks, all dependent on the river for power as well as navigation within the tidal limits.

Up-river the Derwent Iron Company began production in 1841 using local ore and coal. It was succeeded by the Consett Iron Company that went on to dominate the area for many years.

A legendary sporting hero of the area was Harry Clasper, born in nearby Dunston in 1812. The great cult sport in the region of the time was rowing. Harry became champion sculler of the world and enjoyed the kind of hero worship afforded to present day footballers. Before his days of fame he was a Keelman; when he raced tens of thousands would line the river, many placing bets on him to win.

As well as a world-class rower he was an accomplished boat-builder with a business at Derwenthaugh. He invented the outrigger, which transformed the rather clumsy open racing boat to the light rowing skiff of today. Sadly he does not seem to have received recognition for his invention. When he died in 1870 between a hundred and a hundred and thirty thousand mourners watched the funeral cortege pass up river by steam tug to Derwenthaugh prior to his burial in Whickham cemetery.

R.W. THORNTON

Scotswood Bridge

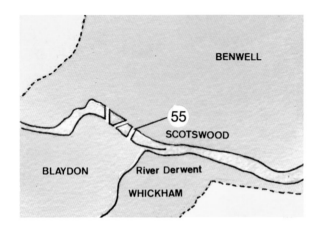

The Scotswood Chain Bridge

As early as 1827, meetings were taking place to discuss the building of a bridge between Lemington and Scotswood on the north side of the river to link with Blaydon on the south. Eventually a company was formed and an Act of Parliament passed to build a road/rail toll bridge.

The directors of the rail company involved lost interest and withdrew from the project, leaving the way for a road bridge only. Work began in 1829 and by 1831 the Chain Suspension Bridge designed by John Green was declared open. It was later to achieve undying fame in the famous Geordie folk song, "The Blaydon Races," ..."we flew across the Chain Bridge reet inter Blaydon toon."

The bridge was opened amid great pomp and ceremony. After the formal procession of carriages packed with local dignitaries had duly crossed, it was estimated that between three and five thousand people surged forward to crowd the bridge. Such a severe test had not been anticipated but to everyone's relief the bridge stood firm. By 1907 the bridge was given county status and tolls ceased.

Not all were enthusiastic however. Once again the Tyne Improvement Commission voiced misgivings; the clearance was too low, even keelboats had to step their masts to gain passage and as a consequence plans for up river development would be in jeopardy. In addition structural problems began to emerge which required significant sums of money for ongoing maintenance. This, along with the dramatic increase in road traffic, resulted in strict speed and weight restrictions. These proved to be the final straw and in 1960 the Department of Transport authorized the building of a replacement bridge.

The new Scotswood Bridge was built slightly up river from its predecessor and opened in 1967. It carries six lanes and was seen as the answer to increased traffic flow for years to come. However it was dogged by bad luck or possibly bad design. Wire cables corroded rapidly, the box-girder design came under suspicion as similar constructions elsewhere in the world using this method had been prone to collapse with significant loss of life. Traffic was severely restricted, reduced to one-way between 1971 and 1974. Major repairs were frequent over the years in an attempt to bring the bridge up to an acceptable standard. At one point it was closed to all vehicles, allowing pedestrian crossing only.

Nobody sings the praises of this bridge.

R.W. THORNTON 2000

Mineral Line - Scotswood

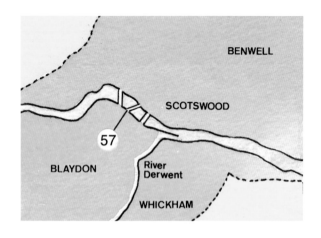

The Hogback Iron Rail Bridge

The existing bridge is the third to be built on the site. In 1829 the Newcastle and Carlisle Rail Co. obtained permission to build a bridge in order to carry rail traffic from the south bank of the river across the Tyne. Until then the Newcastle rail terminus was on the other side of the river at Redheugh.

By 1839, the railway on the Gateshead side was extended west to Blaydon and a bridge link was built across the Tyne to Scotswood and then east to Newcastle. The bridge was designed by the rail company's engineer, John Blackmore, and was meant to be a temporary structure. Unusually it was built at an oblique angle to the course of the river. It was predominantly timber structure except for the abutments, which were of stone. Ten piers, consisting of wooden piles, supported the deck and superstructure.

Over the years increasing disquiet was voiced concerning safety and also that the design presented a major obstruction to navigation. In 1860, engineers from Newcastle and London assisted by the Tyne Improvement Commission carried out an inspection. Their findings were both unanimous and grim! The structure was extremely unsafe and beyond repair. Incredibly, the line remained in use! The only stipulation enforced was that trains were forbidden from crossing the bridge simultaneously. Shortly after the inspection, hot ash presumably from the firebox of a passing engine, fell onto the wooden carriageway, which ignited, destroying the bridge.

1861 saw another temporary wooden bridge erected which remained in place until 1871. In the meantime, the ever-zealous Tyne Improvement Commission had been agitating for a permanent bridge that would allow masted vessels to progress further upstream to aid increased industrial development. They offered substantial financial inducement to help build such a bridge. Their engineer, Mr. Ure, laid out certain requirements: "...the bridge was to be built in a permanent manner that had two opening spans, one on each side of a central pier; that it be made to a proper angle to the river; and generally that it be constructed in such a manner that the navigational interests shall not be sacrificed."

A metal, double-tracked replacement, with wrought iron hog-backed girders supported by cast iron cylindrical piers, was eventually opened in 1871. The design appears to fall significantly short of the Commission's recommendations. The bridge remained in use until 1928. It still stands today, a rather squat, inelegant structure but an interesting remnant of the industrial river.

R. W. Thornton 2000

Blaydon Bridge

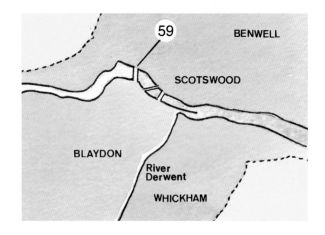

The Western By-Pass - Blaydon

As far back as 1936, the then Ministry of Transport was considering the abolition of all bridge tolls across the Tyne while at the same time introducing a westerly Tyne crossing to relieve increasing traffic congestion in Newcastle. The situation was becoming a problem with the city suffering daily bottlenecks. There was also the added incentive that a new road, reducing traffic flow in residential and commercial areas, would do much to improve the deteriorating environment.

At the time Ministerial suggestions for a new road layout were thought to be a little premature by the local authority, despite the fact that the Scotswood Road Bridge was beginning to raise doubts as to its viability. However, they were persuaded to earmark a corridor of land for future development. This would allow a river crossing at Scotswood, linking up with Blaydon on the south bank.

As the years passed the volume of traffic crossing the river reached a level that required a by-pass. Work began in 1987. Problems were met when previous coal mine workings were exposed that required extensive excavation; over fourteen thousand tonnes of coal were recovered during the process. A further problem was potential traffic noise; much of the new road would run through a densely populated area. This was overcome to a large extent by a combination of a cutting and a "noise wall" barrier. On completion, work then started on he bridge itself and the southern section of the carriageway. The bridge was built using pre-stressed concrete and incorporated an unusual design that uses three balanced cantilevers in parallel – a first in the country.

Yet already the inadequacies of the new highway that carries the re-routed A1 are manifest as traffic density, much boosted by the MetroCentre, can reach four thousand vehicles an hour and cause considerable delays. At least these stoppages give drivers and passengers the opportunity to enjoy the fine views the bridge affords up and down the river.

R.W. THORNTON 2000

Newburn

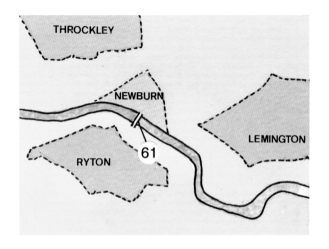

The Boathouse Inn

Newburn was considered to be the tidal limit of the River Tyne. More importantly its three fords were the closest on the river to Newcastle and provided easy crossing long before bridges were built. There are records of crossings as far back as Roman times.

On a number of occasions Scottish armies waded across the river before engaging the English in battle. 1640 witnessed an embarrassing debacle for the English when they were thrashed by the Scots in what became known as, the "The Newburn Rout." To be fair the English were hopelessly outnumbered and had nowhere near the cannon power of their opponents. This ignominious defeat and subsequent occupation of Newcastle was seen as the forerunner to the Civil War. It is said that on the eve of the battle, the Scots issued an invitation to any of the English who cared to cross the river,

to join them in a pre-fight get together: a level of hospitality that beggars belief.

The Percy's acquired Newburn in 1367. At the time it was a thriving community with watermills, a brewery, coal mine, slate quarry and extensive fisheries. By the early nineteenth century there were corn mills, paper mills, coal staithes, chemical works, glass works and iron works as well as extensive coal mining.

Newburn was very much at the centre of the development of the railway. George Stephenson lived here for a while and his two marriages are shown in the local parish records. The tomb of William Hedley, dated 1843, can also be found in the local churchyard. Hedley played a significant part in the development of rail transport but his role has been somewhat overlooked due to the

general acclaim given to Stephenson.

A past link with mining operations in the area was the discovery of the last two remaining Tyne wherries. They lay rotting in river bank mud at Newburn until the late 1950's and probably dated back to the late nineteenth century. Wherries were used to carry coal to waiting ships and were a common sight plying up and down river. Sadly the remains were removed and demolished by a local scrap dealer before their historical significance was realized.

The present iron bridge was built in 1854. Until then a ferry operated from the Boathouse Inn. The bridge was the last on the Tyne to be freed from tolls.

R.W. Thornton 2000

Wylam Road Bridge

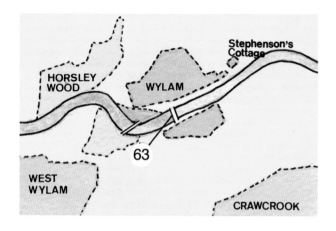

Stephenson's Cottage

The demand for coal during the Industrial Revolution put Wylam firmly on the map. By 1825 the mines and much of the local land were in the possession of the Blackett family. Records at the time show no fewer than five coalmines, two iron works and seven pubs – thirsty work indeed!

As coal owners, the Blacketts showed surprising foresight for the times. Instead of the customary spoil heaps, the waste was reburied in an attempt to preserve the quality of the surrounding countryside.

Christopher Blackett, the squire of Wylam, was the first northern coal owner to realize the potential of the steam locomotive. He actively encouraged local engineers to develop the concept after having experimented unsuccessfully with an engine designed by the Cornishman, Trevithick. In 1812 he tried again with a further prototype, this time assisted by William Hedley from neighbouring Newburn.

Hedley was educated at Wylam. At the age of twenty-two he was appointed manager of Walbottle colliery and later Wylam colliery. The early development of the locomotive relied on a system of cogs, which generated a high level of friction between rail and wheels. Hedley realized that the basic idea was flawed. He worked in great secrecy, often into the night, to develop a smooth rail/wheel system, which he successfully patented in 1813. Thomas Waters, a Gateshead engineer, was commissioned to build a locomotive that proved to be a great success. The engine was named "Puffing Billy", after its designer – presumably meant as a compliment. It was from Wylam colliery that tubs of coal were first hauled along a five-mile stretch of wagonway to the staithes at Lemington.

Despite the heroics of Hedley, Wylam is more widely known as the birthplace of George Stephenson, "The Father of Railways." He designed the "Rocket" and was probably more instrumental than any other in the development of the public railways. George Stephenson was born in 1781 in a humble cottage on the river bank east of Wylam. His father was a miner and George started work at the age of seven; mainly self–taught, he only learned to read at the age of nineteen.

In 1835 the present bridge was built with a roadway provided and a toll charged. The bridge was acquired by the County Council in 1936 and freed from toll charges, although the original toll house still stands on the northwest corner of the bridge. The superstructure of the bridge was renewed and widened in 1960.

R. W. Thornton 2000

Wylam Old Bridge

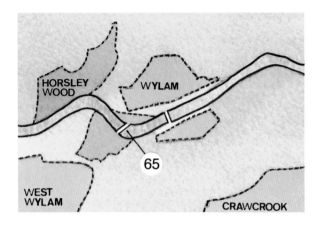

The Old Rail Bridge

By the 1860's pressure had grown in Newcastle to provide a railway west of the city to pass through the industrialized area of Newburn. The Scotswood, Newburn and Wylam Railway Co. received assent from Parliament and in 1872 work began on the six-and-a-half-mile stretch of railway, with work on the bridge commencing in 1874.

William George Laws, consultant engineer for the company, designed the bridge. Originally it was envisaged that the bridge would consist of four spans. The design was discarded when a survey showed that the Tinley coal seam was only thirteen feet below the riverbed. It was feared that if the seam was pierced during the founding of the bridge piers there could be significant structural problems. The revised design consisted of a single arch, formed by three parallel, parabolic, wrought iron lattice ribs and stiffened with cross-bracing abutments. Each end of the bridge was founded in the river bank in cement and built up with masonry. The bridge endured the usual Tyne flood conditions during building and progress was also hampered by a series of minor fires, caused by red hot rivets falling onto the wooden decking.

When completed, the bridge had the distinction of being the first single-arch bridge built for a railway crossing. There are also design echoes in the Tyne and Sydney Harbour bridges, which were to follow half a century later. Wylam Bridge was built to a new design and the stringency of the tests prior to the formal opening reflected this. They were formidable and were carried out under the watchful eye of Colonel Hutchinson from the Board of Trade. Proceedings commenced with a thirty-six ton locomotive plus a twenty-five ton tender crossing the bridge at speed. Then a further forty-five ton locomotive was coupled up and the crossing repeated. Finally six locomotives and tenders were coupled together and driven across the bridge repeatedly. On successful completion of the tests, "with little or no deflection observed", the Colonel had the good grace to praise the rail crew for their bravery in the face of danger, "which had been apprehended by all." There is no record of the crew's comments at the close of their ordeal. The bridge was closed to rail traffic in 1968 and has since become a popular, well-maintained footpath and cycle track. It now provides an attractive and apposite link across the river to the cottage where George Stephenson was born.

Prudhoe and Ovingham

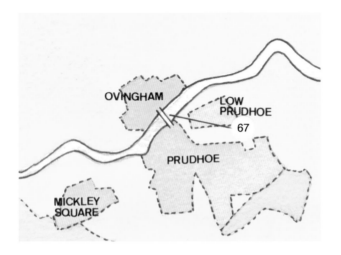

Prudhoe Castle

The church and vicarage on the north bank of the river and Prudhoe Castle on the south bank dominate the skyline here. Rumours have long persisted that an underwater tunnel links the vicarage with Prudhoe but evidence has yet to come to light. This particular stretch of the Tyne was often difficult to cross because of the turbulence caused by the rocky and uneven riverbed. Daily life along the riverbank was significantly affected by this restriction, despite the fact that at one time there were no fewer than five ferries and eight fords between Bywell and Ovingham.

Locals had clamoured for the building of a bridge to link the two communities for literally centuries, all to no avail. One persistent campaigner was no other than Thomas Bewick, the acclaimed engraver. Born and living in Cherryburn but educated across the river in Ovingham, he made an impassioned plea in the Newcastle Courant in 1816, using the nom de plume, "The Hermit of Horsley Wood". Why a hermit would seek a bridge to increase communication is a little puzzling! In his submission, Bewick had the temerity to suggest that a bridge would please the locals far more than a proposed monument extolling the virtues of the then Duke of Northumberland. No wonder he chose not to reveal his identity. Once again the plea fell on deaf ears.

It was not until 1883 that a bridge was eventually built. The relief felt must have been tempered by the fact that a toll was levied, which was not lifted until 1945. The tollhouse is still in place adjacent to Prudhoe rail station. A separate footbridge was eventually built downstream of the main bridge in 1974.

The dramatic setting of Prudhoe Castle was chosen with care to take full advantage of the land's natural defence. The castle, considered impregnable, was for many years in the capable hands of the Umfravilles. It is one of a select band of fortifications nationwide never to have been breached. King William of Scotland invaded twice in 1173 and 1174 without success. In what can only be described as a fit of pique, it was reported that the retreating army devastated the surrounding countryside, laying waste to cornfields and even stripping the bark from apple trees. Over the years the castle fell into disrepair but was considerably altered and restored by the Duke of Northumberland in the early nineteenth century. It is now in the care of English Heritage.

R. W. Thornton 2000

Bywell

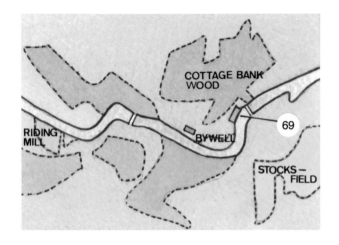

St Peter's Church

Bywell, thirteen miles west of Newcastle, lies in a beautiful setting on the north bank of the Tyne where the river makes a wide, gentle curve between overhanging wooded banks. A fifteenth century ivy-clad castle, a handsome manor house set in parkland, two churches and a handful of stone houses offer a haven of peace and tranquillity rarely found today.

This was not always the case; in the sixteenth century Bywell was a sizeable village and one of the busiest communities in the Tyne valley. Its churches, some twenty dwellings, several shops, a market, an inn and several small businesses ensured a thriving, bustling community. The area was particularly noted for craftsmen who produced a range of ironware; including stirrups, bridles, buckles, and armour for horsemen. The constant

Border warfare that kept the ironworkers busy also meant an uncertain life for the inhabitants of Bywell. Every evening they were forced to herd their cattle into the main street, where they were guarded until the morning.

The building of the castle, under the authority of Ralph de Neville second Earl of Westmorland, began in 1426 but was never completed. One possible explanation was that the Umfravilles, who held the nearby barony of Prudhoe, were jealous of their power base and successfully petitioned King Henry III to oppose further building. The castle was virtually a gate tower protected by a portcullis, the retaining grooves still visible in the stonework. It was to this castle that Henry VI fled for shelter following defeat in the Battle of Hexham during the War of the Roses, only just managing to evade

the clutches of his enemies and leaving behind his crown, sword and helmet.

It is something of a puzzle as to why such a small community should contain two churches so close to each other. Legend has it that they were built by quarrelling sisters merely to prove a point. A more prosaic explanation is that they were built near coinciding boundaries of two parishes. At one time St. Andrew belonged to the White Canons of Blanchland and St. Peter to the Benedictine Monastery of Durham. St. Peter still serves the parishioners of Stocksfield, whilst the Church of St. James at nearby Riding Mill has usurped St. Andrew, now declared redundant.

R.W. THORNTON 2000

Bywell Estate

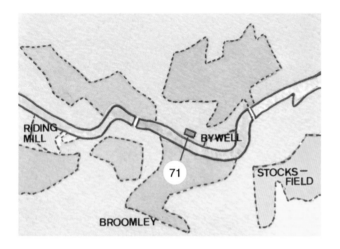

St Andrew's Church

In 1569, the Bywell estate came into the possession of the Crown. As a result the grounds gradually fell into disrepair. The renowned woodlands were plundered for timber; salmon and deer poaching were widespread and buildings were neglected. To rid himself of this far-flung problem James I granted the barony to Sir John Fenwick of nearby Wallington.

Bywell Hall was built in 1766 by William Fenwick and designed by James Paine, an architect of national importance. It was erected on the base of an earlier building and built in the Palladian style with an Ionic portico.

The Great Flood of 1771 devastated Bywell. A number of lives were lost and many buildings destroyed. A story of the time tells of Mary Leighton, a little girl who was swept away in her wooden cradle, only to be found alive and well at the mouth of the Tyne

Possession of Bywell by the Fenwicks ended in 1802 and in 1809 the estate was sold to the lead mining magnate of Allendale, Thomas Wentworth. During this period the river could only be crossed by ford or ferry although there is evidence of a bridge, possibly Roman, downriver from the castle. The remains consist of two solid stone piers that may have supported a wooden carriageway. In 1836 the ancient bridge piers were blown up (killing one worker, seriously injuring another) prior to the laying of a foundation for a new bridge.

The new bridge, opened in 1838 was a handsome affair with five stone arches; the entire cost was borne by Mr. T.W. Beaumont. He was widely praised for allowing free public passage, highly unusual in a toll-conscious era. Despite strong local opposition from his neighbours the same Mr. Beaumont supported the proposed new railway from Newcastle to Carlisle. The fact that the railway would have considerably assisted the transportation of lead from his mines in Alston may have had some bearing upon his outlook. Nevertheless he still insisted that the line be hidden from view of the Hall in a cutting.

R.W. Thornton 2000

Styford Bridge

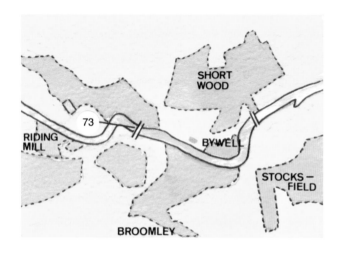

Riding Mill - Styford Bridge

Styford bypass was planned to relieve the rapidly increasing flow of traffic through Riding Mill and Corbridge. Prior to its construction traffic from the A68 had to descend the notoriously steep Whiteside Bank into the small village of Riding Mill whether it was going east towards Newcastle or west towards Corbridge. After many years campaigning a new road was built, with an elegant bridge, supported on slender oval piers, crossing the Tyne.

The relief was immediate; overnight Riding Mill returned to being a pleasant quiet village. Drivers were also pleased to have been freed from the dangers of the steep descent and the inconvenience of a narrow built-up road.

An incident that attracted national publicity for Riding Mill occurred in 1990 when two RAF jets collided over the village. The wreckage from one of the aircraft hurtled through the up-stream parapet, bounced on to the bridge and then tore through the down-stream parapet. Not many bridges have been closed due to falling aircraft! Fortunately the aircrew survived the accident.

72

R.W. Thornton 2000

Riding Mill Pumping Station

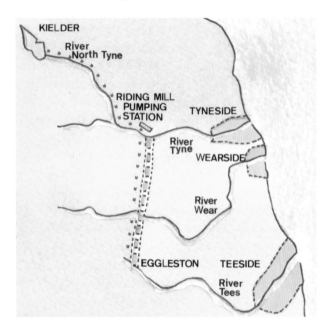

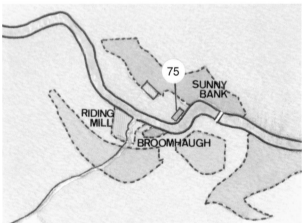

The Weir

The Kielder Water Scheme was designed to supply water to Tyneside, Wearside and Teesside over eighty miles away. The scheme allowed water to be stored at Kielder reservoir and then released by means of a valve control tower. The route did not follow a straight line but took advantage of the existing river systems, travelling thirty-six miles from the dam through the River North Tyne and the Tyne itself and finally to a pumping station at Riding Mill to be transferred south.

The transfer works were an essential part of the scheme. The site was chosen at Riding Mill because it provided one of the shortest links with Eggleston on the River Tees. The river at this point was also eminently suitable for extraction because it has a deep natural pool. When completed it was the largest pumping station of its type in the United Kingdom, housing huge pumps capable of lifting water seven hundred feet up the valley to Letch House, the highest point in the system four miles away. From this point the water would then flow south by gravity in concrete lined tunnels down to the River Tees. In addition to the pumping station a weir was constructed two hundred yards downstream, providing a minimum water level in order to control water release down the Tyne. A fish pass was also built near the south bank, which allowed fish to move upstream past the dam in order to reach their spawning grounds.

Understandably, the project raised concerns with the residents of Riding Mill a mere quarter of a mile away who were anxious about the effect of a large building on the environment, the potential damage to property due to underground vibration and the possibility of overhead electricity pylons. The Water Authority gave assurances and were as good as their word; tree planting and landscaping virtually hide the building from view, the electricity cables were laid underground, the anticipated noise never materialised and the fish pass proved to be too successful – at times poachers could lift the fish out by hand (padlocks have now been fitted to prevent this). The only real casualty was the loss of the historic ford upstream, linking Styford with Broomhaugh.

R.W. Thornton 2001

Styford Hall

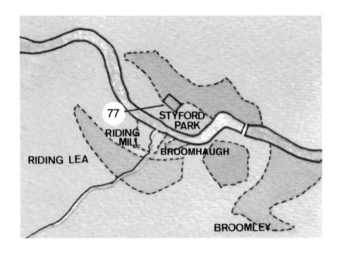

Styford Hall Stables

After the Norman Conquest the ancient earldom of Northumberland was split into several baronies. One of these was Styford. An inquiry in 1262 mentions a mill, a chapel and the barony court, as well as woodland from which timber was sold for charcoal. The 'township' stretched two miles to the north from the riverbank opposite Riding Mill.

The township was destroyed in 1346, when David, King of Scots laid waste to much of south Northumberland. Only a conical mound, which was once a defensive motte now remains. John Bacon acquired the estate in 1708. The family built the present five-bay house and handsome stable block just over a century later. The estate, with two others, eventually passed to a surviving daughter Emily, who in turn left it to a cousin, a diplomat Sir Percy Lorrain whom she had never met. He was naturally thrilled and wrote, "I have just become a Northumberland landowner and you can imagine what an agreeable feeling that is."

He first saw his properties in 1921 then chose to make Styford his residence because of the fine fishing on the Tyne and his close friendship with the Cuthbert family in nearby Beaufront Castle. The 1901 Census records a population of more than seventy in Styford; including the farms and cottages at Brockbushes and High Barns. Although Sir Percy often visited the Hall, his diplomatic duties made it much less than a permanent home. A keen man of the turf, he named one of his racehorses 'Styford'.

The Hall was rented from Sir Percy in 1918 to Robert Dickinson, a Newcastle solicitor. His groom (James) used to row him across the river to Riding Mill to catch the train to work. His five sons and daughters would later recall idyllic childhood days picnicking and fishing on the river bank, playing tennis and enjoying the gardens and grounds.

R.W.Thornton 2001

Corbridge

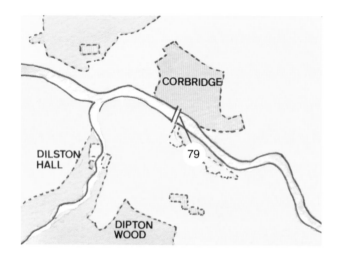

The Bridge Approach

Corbridge on the north bank of the Tyne was once one of the most important towns in Northumberland. In Roman times it was a major supply base and trade centre. The Roman bridge was near the Cor Burn, half a mile above the present one. The remains of the abutments and piers can still be seen when the river is low.

After the demise of the Roman bridge the river was crossed by a ford. Located a few hundred yards below the present bridge, it was reached by a path from the east end of Main Street. In 1235 the burgesses of Corbridge built a new bridge to link their side of the river with Simon of Divelston's land, paying him a pound of pepper and a pound of cumin annually.

In 1666 the citizens of Newcastle complained that the bridge was "ruined and in decay" and so was damaging trade. The county authorities set about building the present bridge, which has the date 1674 chiselled into it. Soundly designed and constructed, this bridge alone survived the Great Flood of 1771, perhaps because the waters found their way over the low-lying ground of Dilston Eals.

The bridge was always narrow for wheeled traffic and so was widened in 1881 to allow carriages to pass. For a time in the 1970s an ugly modern girder bridge stood alongside the old bridge. It was removed after the Hexham/Corbridge bypass was completed, leaving the handsome old seven-arched landmark, to be admired by visitors to Tynedale.

The Old Smithy

R.W. THORNTON 2001

Beaufront Castle

The East Wing

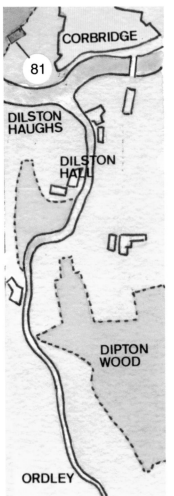

Beaufront Castle was the seat of the Carnabys in the reign of Queen Elizabeth. Later it passed into the hands of the Errington family who built a large prominent mansion overlooking the Tyne. There can be few more imposing settings within the area, with far reaching views that follow the meandering course of the river. Directly opposite across the river is Dilston Hall, the seat of James Radcliffe, third Earl of Derwentwater. It is recorded that at one time the two used to communicate across the valley by means of a speaking trumpet.

Beaufront was associated with both the fortunes and misfortunes of the Earl of Derwentwater. In 1715, the Earl visited Beaufront in attempt to persuade Errington to join him in the Jacobite Rebellion. Errington took him by the arm and led him to the walls of the house and pointed to the expansive Dilston estates and asked him if was really prepared to risk such a fine inheritance for such a doubtful cause. The rest is history! Errington was sympathetic however, as a short time later he hid the Earl under an oak staircase to escape from government agents.

After John Errington's death in 1827 the house fell into disrepair. William Cuthbert bought the estate; in 1835 he demolished a large part of the building and erected the present 'castle'. Designed by John Dobson, the eminent Newcastle architect, it is an imposing castellated structure. Dobson apparently considered it to be his finest achievement. The building work led to the re-opening of a nearby quarry and a rail system was brought in from Meldon Hall near Morpeth. The system consisted of wooden rails carrying horse-drawn wagons. At one time an unbelievable two hundred men were said to be working on the site. Where did they come from? Where did they live? When excavating the foundations a large Roman mosaic was discovered but reburied.

A stream with the misleading name of 'Devils Water' flows into the Tyne directly opposite Beaufront. This most attractive stretch of water travels from the Allendale moors, past the old Dipton Mill, tumbling noisily over rocky outcrops before flowing under the Hexham road bridge to the low-lying Dilston haughs.

R.W. Thornton 2001

Hexham

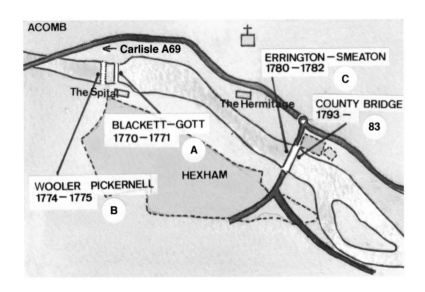

The Abbey and Market Square

Hexham was not an obvious site to build a bridge, set well back on a high terrace, overlooking a broad flood plain. In the thirteenth century there was a bridge probably built of wood which fell into disrepair and was eventually abandoned. For centuries after, the only means of crossing was by ford or ferry.

The mid eighteenth century saw rapid industrial growth and the need for a bridge became pressing. In 1775 James Jurin inherited the Hermitage on the north bank opposite Hexham and persuaded his friend, John Smeaton, then an up and coming civil engineer to design a road bridge. Smeaton supplied a design, but Jurin died and Sir Walter Blackett who owned the estate of Hexham took over the reins and employed William Gott to design

a bridge. Money was raised by public subscription and in 1767 the first stone was laid (A) just under a mile from the present bridge. The bridge had only been open a year when the Great Flood of 1771 struck and the bridge collapsed.

Undeterred, Blackett approached Smeaton who showed little interest, but his assistant, John Wooler accepted the commission. Work began in 1774 a short distance up river from the Gott disaster (B), but the project was abandoned almost immediately when the river bed was found to be totally unsuitable. A more promising location was selected down river at Sandhoe on Henry Errington's estate, who undertook to finance the bridge and approached Smeaton, who this time agreed. Work commenced in 1777 but was

interrupted by flood damage, forcing Smeaton to reconsider his design. Three years later the bridge (C) opened to considerable acclaim and wild celebration. It did not last long; in March 1782 dreadful floods destroyed the bridge in less than half an hour. The eminent Smeaton was distraught.

Eventually the County's own surveyors, Robert Thompson and William Johnson were entrusted to rebuild the bridge on the same site. Robert Mylne who had been responsible for a number of successful bridges in the area, was called in to supervise the building work. The county bridge has survived both river and traffic flow and is still in use today.

Hexham Tyne Green

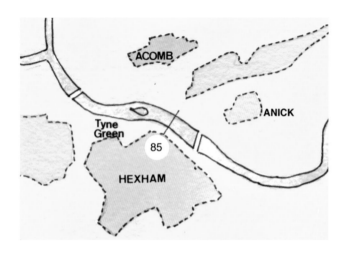

County Bridge and view West towards Tyne Green

Tyne Green is a broad flood plain lying on the south bank of the river below Hexham. Over the years the Green became a thriving community of market gardeners, fruit growers and allied craftsmen.

Since the fourteenth century, annual fairs lasting several days were held on the Green where dealing in livestock and leather goods mainly took place.

Tyne Green was an obvious point to cross the river, at first by two fords. The High Ford was the busier and considered the more dangerous of the two. It was approached via Gillesgate before crossing the river to Acomb. From here there was a route up the North Tyne Valley to Chollerton and on towards Alnmouth where grain was exported. Other travellers would venture down Hallstile Bank and cross by the Low Ford, near the site of the present bridge, to head eastwards.

The Hermitage on the opposite side of the river to Hexham had some interesting occupants. It takes its name from a supposed link with St. John of Beverley who is said to have sought solitude there whilst he was Bishop of Hexham. In the eighteenth century the Jurins were occupants. James Jurin was the Master of Newcastle Grammar School before switching to medicine.

Until 1886 the lord of the manor held the mineral rights of Tyne Green while the commoners held grazing rights. The town took over in 1887 and converted the Green to leisure use. The rowing club is one of the oldest clubs in the northeast, there is now a golf course laid out and in recent years the riverbank has become a Country Park.

The Constantium Bridge

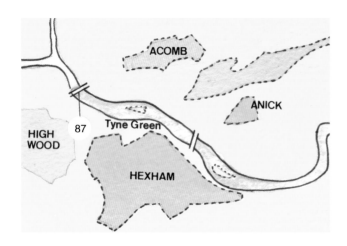

Kingshaw Green

To relieve traffic from Hexham the decision was made to build an eight-and-a-half mile by-pass along the north bank of the Tyne. While many welcomed the scheme, others were concerned at the effect on Cor Burn and the Hermitage Park. The decision was made to erect a bridge at Kingshaw Green below the Meeting of the Waters. Apparently as surveyors were examining the river bed to find a suitable location to site the concrete piers, they were accosted by two aged ex-Acomb miners walking their dogs. With a great deal of head shaking they passed on their view that "This was nee place to build bridges, it had been tried before". The experts decided to ignore the advice and preparations went ahead. Initially a temporary bridge was constructed with steel piles and timber crossbeams, to enable the workforce of

two hundred and plant to cross the river. A flash flood damaged the structure, sweeping away a number of cross beams – an ominous event. A year later turbulent floodwater scoured the gravel and sand from around the concrete piers; over a hundred sheets of wooden shuttering ended up downriver. Come back Smeaton, all is forgiven. The bridge was eventually completed, but has required later remedial and strengthening work to protect against periodic flooding.

A short distance downstream are the remains of a much earlier river crossing. The stumps of the old wooden piers of the Border Counties Rail Bridge can still be seen straddling the river. This was once an important junction, carrying the branch line from the Newcastle-Carlisle railway up the North

Tyne Valley to Kielder and Hawick. It suffered flood damage in 1856 and once again almost a century later; finally it was destroyed by explosives after Dr. Beeching closed the line.

Kingshaw Green is no stranger to bypasses. In 1745 General Wade set out from Newcastle to intercept Jacobites attempting to cross the border at Carlisle. En route they encountered dreadful road conditions. On reaching Kingshaw Green the route west was impassable. Frustrated, Wade abandoned his march and returned to Newcastle, where he pressed for an alternative east-west route. Shortly afterwards the Military Road 'by-pass' now the B6318 was constructed.

R.W. THORNTON 2001

The Meeting of the Waters

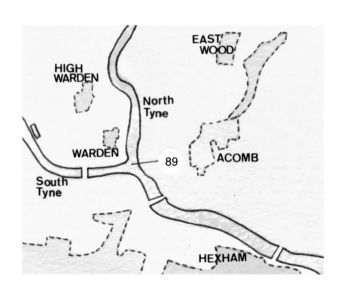

The Confluence of the Tynes

A vast area of over a thousand square miles of land drains into the River Tyne; from the peat moorland and lead dales of Cross Fell to the conifer hills of Kielder where the Pennine and Cheviot Hills merge. The South and North Tyne meet at Warden Rock, a place that is known as the 'meeting of the waters'. The South Tyne has travelled thirty-nine miles over boulder strewn beds and constantly-shifting islands of gravel, while the North Tyne has enjoyed a more sedate journey of some forty miles through wide valley and flood plains. From the confluence the main Tyne flows a further thirty-two miles to the mouth of the river.

Heavy and prolonged rainfall over Alston Moor and Kielder often results in both rivers meeting in full spate, which is a spectacular sight. The Tyne has the dubious distinction of having the highest ever-recorded flood flow of any river in England and Wales, when a flow of sixteen hundred tons of water per second was recorded at Bywell. This equates to a velocity of eleven miles per hour on unrestricted stretches of river, but when confined by bridges and other obstacles it can be considerably greater. It explains why bridge building at Hexham was so difficult. When John Smeaton was approached to rebuild his failed bridge at Hexham he replied:

"I would beg you to consider whether you may not stand a better chance by employing some other able engineer who has not got the horrors of the River Tyne painted upon his imagination."

The North Tyne

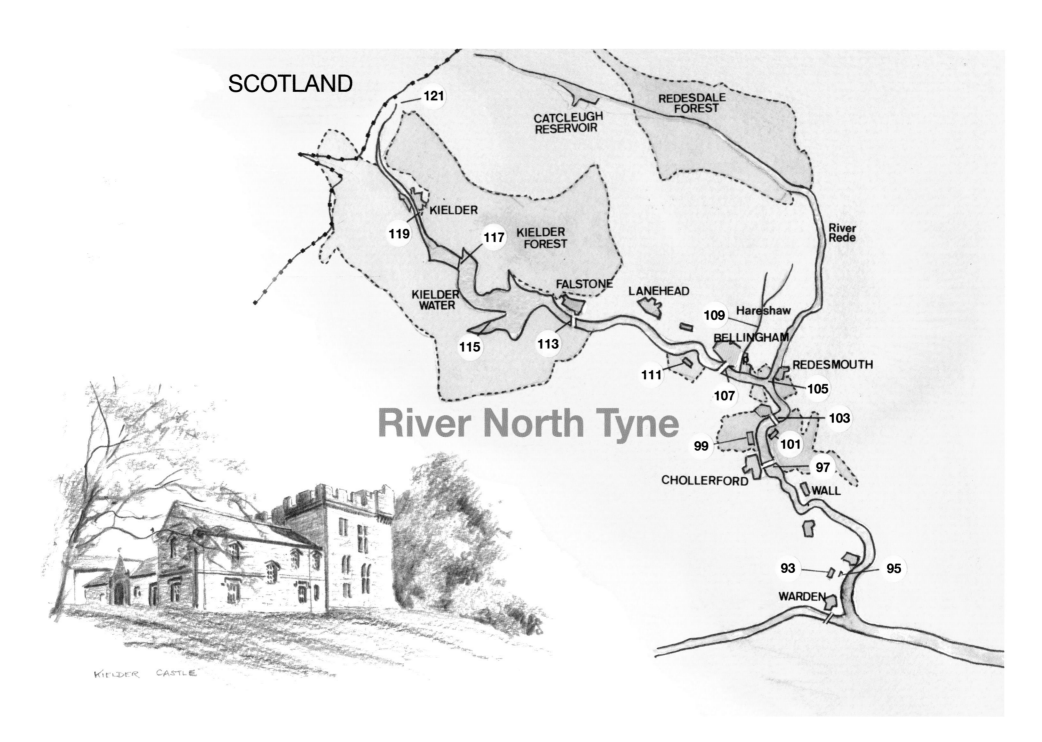

SCOTLAND

121

CATCLEUGH
RESERVOIR

REDESDALE
FOREST

KIELDER

119   KIELDER
           FOREST   117

KIELDER
WATER

FALSTONE   LANEHEAD

                              109   Hareshaw

115   113

                    BELLINGHAM

                              REDESMOUTH

111

                              105

107

River North Tyne   103

99   101

                              97

CHOLLERFORD

                    WALL

River
Rede

93   95

WARDEN

KIELDER CASTLE

Chesters

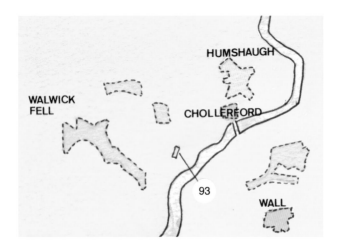

The West Wing

The first recorded building was a camp built by Agricola in 78 AD but the main post dates from the time of Hadrian. although much altered over the centuries and robbed out later for building stone. The bath-house, close to the river, is one of the best preserved examples in Britain.

The estate passed to the Erringtons in the sixteenth century. In 1740 John Errington added a "modern structure' to the old tower house but this was replaced in 1770 by a fine house build by John Carr of York.

Nathaniel Clayton, Town Clark of Newcastle from 1785-1822 bought the estate in 1796 and laid out the park. His son John Clayton, who succeeded his father as Town Clerk in 1822 and held the post until 1867, was not only an eminent lawyer, influ-ential on many local bodies, but an enthusiastic antiquarian who gradually bought up any Roman sites which came on the market until his estates stretched as far as Vindolanda. Clayton also per-suaded people not to destroy walls and forts by taking stones for buildings and roads. He exca-vated much of the Roman Fort and built up a large collection of Roman antiquities until the house and garden resembled a museum.

John Clayton was one of eleven children, there the family fertility ceased and on his death in 1890 the estate was inherited by his nephew Nathaniel, son of his younger brother the Rev. Richard Clayton.

Nathaniel at once set about enlarging the house and employed R. Norman Shaw as his architect, who added two splendid (if oversized) curved wings, a North forecourt and the cheerful neo-Baroque sta-ble block across the main and in 1896 a museum to house the cream of John Clayton's collection.

In its heyday Chesters employed thirty-eight indoor servants and no less than sixteen gardeners. On Clayton's death the house and part of the estate were sold to Alexander Kieth and over the over the next few years Mrs Keith redesigned most of the garden.

However the old garden wall, the fine steps and curved hedges in front of the house remain as they were. The house and grounds are now owned by the Benson family and the Roman fort is in the care of English Heritage.

R.W. Thornton 2001

Chesters Roman Fort

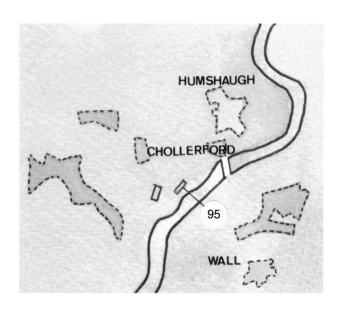

The Bath House

The North Tyne flows under Chollerford Bridge to Chesters, one of the most important Roman sites in Britain; Cilurnum reputed to have been built by Agricola in 81AD. Hadrian's Wall was the official frontier for many centuries and originally ran through the centre of the site. The cavalry fort was adjacent to the river and thus commanded the valley of Tynedale.

The Wall and the road were carried over the river by a bridge built in the third century. When the river level is low the eastern abutment of the bridge can still be seen. The remains are an outstanding example of Roman building skills, exposing large, dressed pieces of stone linked by iron clamps ingeniously embedded in lead.

Apparently the camp reputation was superior to others along the Wall. The location of the fort in tree-lined meadows sloping gently down towards the river and encircled by hills which served to keep out the worst of the Northumbrian rain and winds, coupled with the excellent hunting and fishing, made Chesters the place to be. The clinching factor was undoubtedly the garrison bathhouse – claimed to be the finest military bathhouse of its time in Britain.

Visitors can examine the layout of this multi-purpose building with its changing rooms, hot, cold and warm bathing areas; steam baths and massage rooms. The system was fed by a series of hot air underfloor and cavity-wall channels continuously heated by three stoke holes.

This was undoubtedly the hub of garrison life, resembling a mix of NAAFI , sauna, Turkish bath and social club. It was an ideal place to meet in luxurious comfort to moan about the weather, the food, superior officers, the locals and most importantly, gossip from home.

Chollerford

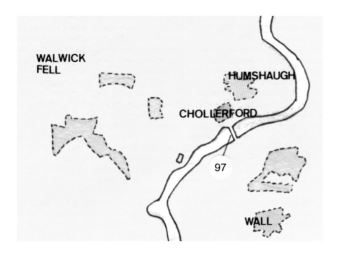

The Weir

As the name suggests, the North Tyne was crossed here by means of a ford, the precise location of which has not been identified. It is hardly more than a bridge and a hotel.

Before the construction of the present bridge there was an earlier bridge, some two or three yards downstream. This bridge, like many others, became a victim of the Great Flood of 1771 and was completely demolished. The present bridge was built in 1775 and is a substantial structure widely admired for its five (instead of the previous four) arches; a lesson learned from the previous disaster. 1976 saw the road over the bridge narrowed and lights were installed to regulate the single file traffic.

The first recorded reference to the George goes back to 1769. An early map shows two separate buildings, one being the inn and the other possibly a boathouse from which a ferry may have operated. The earliest part of the present building dates from the early to mid eighteenth century and was apparently called the New Inn. It was reputedly built with stone purloined from neighbouring Roman sites – a widespread practice at the time.

In 1776 a local newspaper carried the story of a stork that was shot at Chollerford, the skin being nailed upon the wall of the inn. Crowds flocked to see the sight, giving rise to a roaring trade – the power of advertising has long been a potent force.

W. Hutchinson in his View of Northumberland 1778, certainly enjoyed the hospitality offered and wrote;

"The inn at Chollerford tempted our stay – A spacious room built for the resort of the neighbouring gentlemen afforded us a pleasing view of the river; whilst excellent accommodation indulged us with that degree of satisfaction, which truly constitutes the traveller's ease."

The George at Chollerford is now a grand affair but until the 1960s was little more than a wayside inn. Three of its many literary visitors in the past include; WH Auden, George Bernard Shaw and Rudyard Kipling.

R.W. Thornton 2001

Haughton Castle

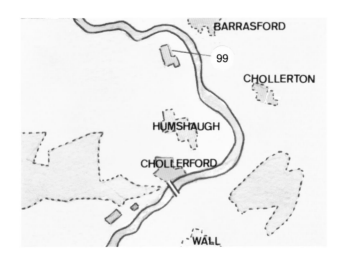

Haughton Castle

Haughton Castle stands among tall pines overlooking one the most beautiful stretches of the North Tyne River. This medieval stronghold was first mentioned in 1373 as a county gentleman's dwelling. Considering that the occupant of that time was William de Swinburne, a well-known local bully who laid dubious claims to neighbouring lands, such a title would appear rather euphemistic.

During its turbulent history the building was gradually converted into a castle, thereby losing much of its grace and beauty. After repeated attacks it was deserted and fell to ruins.

In 1751 it passed into the hands of William Smith, a retired sea captain dubbed "The Buccaneer". Smith began the long overdue task of restoration while occupying a small section of the building. He enclosed the park and built a walled garden. His improvements to the parkland unfortunately lead to the flattening of a number of cottages housing some two hundred people.

The hapless inhabitants were sent packing to nearby Humshaugh. He installed a sundial in the grounds inscribed, "Haughton Castle 1796" which consisted of a number of small dials representing the foreign ports with which he was familiar. He took great delight in arranging the dials to show the correct time in each port.

In 1888 Mr. Cruddas, a local industrialist purchased Haughton and did much to help the castle return to its former glory.

During the reign of Henry II a ferry was introduced, connecting Haughton with the village of Barrasford. The ferry was operated by a rope and pulley system that survived for a remarkable seven hundred years before it was discontinued in the mid-1970's. This ferry was one of several sites claiming to be the origin of the famous Northumbrian folk song, "The Water of Tyne." Naturally Haughton has its ghost story. Sir Thomas Swinburne had incarcerated the local clan chieftain, Archie Armstrong for "cattle – lifting" and was then summoned immediately to York on urgent business. After three days on horseback he arrived to discover that the only keys to Haughton's dungeon were attached to his girdle. Showing unusual compassion for the times, he called for fresh horses and returned poste-haste only to find poor Archie dead. In extremes of hunger Archie had gnawed the flesh from his forearms before his death. It is recorded that for many years after his death, dreadful screams echoed throughout the castle until his ghost was eventually exorcised.

R.W. Thornton 2001

Chipchase Castle

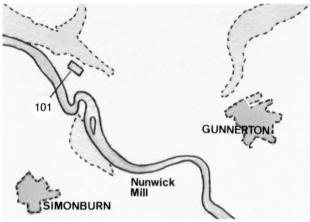

Georgian Splendour

Chipchase Castle is regarded as one of the most stately and picturesque of the Northumbrian mansions although there is some dispute about the derivation of its name. Some historians maintain that it comes from the Anglo Saxon, "chepan", to buy and sell and the French, "chasse", for hunting grounds. Hence Chipchase, a market within a hunting area. Others claim a little less romantic background from the words "cip", a log and "kos", an animal trap made of timber.

The grounds retain the foundation stones from a lost Anglo-Saxon village important enough at one time to have been a market site. In the mid thirteenth century Chipchase was held by the Umfravilles of Prudhoe as a detached manor providing rich hunting grounds. A fort was built to the south of the present castle in order to protect the village. The estate passed into the Lisle family, then in 1384 Cecily de Lisle married Walter Heron of Ford and thus the Herons, a redoubtable Border family came to Chipchase.

In 1621 Cuthbert Heron added a Jacobean mansion to the original pele tower. The result was acclaimed as the finest seventeenth century house in the whole of Northumberland; containing fine rooms, large windows and carved mantelpieces. Cuthbert Heron was created a baronet for his loyalty to Charles II in 1662.

During the years of Border unrest the Herons were frequently appointed Keepers of Tynedale, an important position directly responsible to the Wardens of the English Middle Marches for the upkeep of law and order in the region. Chipchase could only house fifty men for mounted patrols in the area, rather a small garrison in view of the turbulent times.

Apparently not all the Herons were as mindful of their civic duty. "Little John" Heron sought to capitalize on Henry VIII's scourge of the church by gathering around him a gang of ruffians whom he offered as paid guardians to the threatened canons of Hexham Priory. To make this offer more attractive he tried at the same time to incite royal reprisal against the canons whose wealth and suspected "treasonable attitude" had been reported to the king. The canons, already shielded by the militantly protective stance of local folk, rejected his overtures and Heron acquired the soubriquet "Crafty John".

The Herons owned the Castle and estate from 1348-1695. They were sold by Sir Harry, the last of the Herons, at the end of the sevententh. century. The Chipchase estate then passed through the hands of several local families, including the Allgoods, Reeds (who built the chapel facing the Jacobean front) and the Greys. It was purchased in 1862 by Lt. Col. Taylor and today remains the family home of his descendant Penelope Taylor.

R.W. THORNTON 2001

Wark

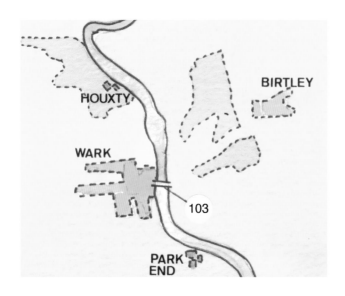

Wark Village

Wark, pronounced Ark, Old English for fort or fortification, is a small village nestling on the bank of the North Tyne and enjoys a lineage totally belaying its modest appearance. Handsome stone buildings flank an attractive village green, dominated by a magnificent chestnut tree planted to celebrate the Golden Jubilee of Queen Victoria.

The village green is common land beside which travellers may rest up to twenty-four hours before moving on. Close by, an iron bridge crosses the river, replacing a hazardous, wooden structure unpopular with the locals who also objected to the toll system; a penny per person, two pence for a horse and cart. As a result many still opted to use the sometimes-dangerous ford crossing downstream.

On approaching the village from the south there is a hill believed to be the site of an old Norman motte and bailey castle. The motte was levelled to build the present farm; all that remains is a Tudor stone lintel above the main door. In medieval times Wark enjoyed great importance and was acknowledged as the "Capitol" of North Tynedale, with the Courts of Liberty of Tynedale being held here. Wark, then consisted of a prison, fulling mill, corn mill, brewery, forge, bakehouse and large deer parks. The ancient court had existed since the early Middle Ages and still functioned as late as 1883, under the grandiose title of, " The Court Leet and View of Frankpledge." Leet meaning the list of people entitled to be present and Frankpledge meaning each representative of an approved region responsible for the good conduct of its citizens.

Giles Heron, the illegitimate son of one of the Herons of Chipchase, established one of the earliest schools in the area at Wark in 1684. He was a peddler by trade but by combining hard work and self-denial was able to amass a fortune of eight hundred pounds - his sales technique must have been something to behold. He was eventually persuaded to use the money to found a school for poor children in the area.

Another local character was Abel Chapman, a famous naturalist who purchased a dilapidated sheep farm close to Wark. He renovated the buildings and created extensive gardens and plantations. He often travelled abroad and on his return wrote many books and articles describing the flora and fauna he encountered; he also presented numerous specimens to various local museums. He died in 1929 and is buried in the churchyard at Wark.

Redeswater

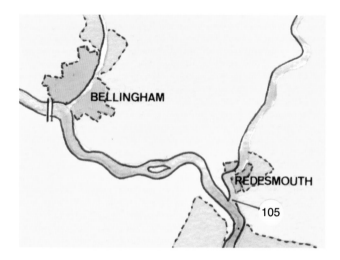

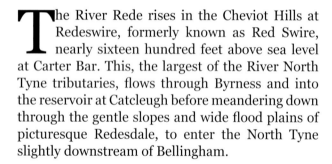

Catcleugh Reservoir Outlet

The River Rede rises in the Cheviot Hills at Redeswire, formerly known as Red Swire, nearly sixteen hundred feet above sea level at Carter Bar. This, the largest of the River North Tyne tributaries, flows through Byrness and into the reservoir at Catcleugh before meandering down through the gentle slopes and wide flood plains of picturesque Redesdale, to enter the North Tyne slightly downstream of Bellingham.

Redesdale for many centuries was a lawless area; its inhabitants were notorious for their skill in "night-riding" and indulging in a little "shifting" for their living. Most not only robbed and plundered but boasted of their exploits in the local taverns. They raised their children to regard all forms of stealing as an art rather than a crime. In a vain attempt to prevent reiving, special watches were kept at night over every river ford in the Rede Valley.

Like their North Tynedale neighbours, the district was dominated by families or graynes, the most notorious being the Reeds. Typical of the times, Percy Reed was appointed as Keeper of Redesdale to oversee law and order within the area – a classic example of, "running with the hare and hunting with the hounds." By all accounts he discharged his duties with fearless vigour and was described as a great hunter and fighter, rude of speech, contemptuous of religion and restraint: an impressive curriculum vitae for the time! He was waylaid by the Crosier/Halls who, before leaving him to die, hacked off his hands and feet!

At the time border law allowed victims of reiving up to six days to set out in pursuit. They carried pieces of burning turf attached to lances to show that their action was lawful. This was known as, "hot trod," hence hot foot in pursuit.

The Rede was eventually dammed to form Catcleugh Reservoir from which water was piped down to Hallington and then on to Whittle Dene, near Stamfordham, to provide water for the population of Tyneside. Work started in 1889, the reservoir finally being filled in 1906. The name, Catcleugh, is derived from the wild cats that once roamed the small gullies or cleughs that criss-cross the steep valley sides.

The reservoir was virtually dug out by shovel and pick, a vast undertaking. Most of the labour force was recruited from Newcastle and Gateshead. To prevent outbreaks of violence, a long-standing problem due to centuries of cross-Tyne feuding, two separate "villages" were set up on opposite banks of the Rede; one designated Newcastle and the other Gateshead. However all the children were taught in the same school at Byrness; this must have kept the teaching staff on their toes. In the church over looking the river is a window commemorating the sixty-four who died during the reservoir's construction.

R.W. Thornton 2001

Bellingham

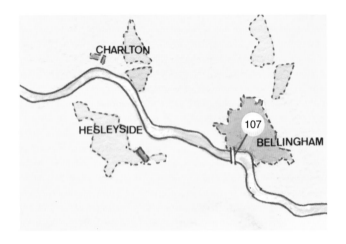

The Market Place

Pronounced "Bellinjum" for non-Northumbrians, the town lies alongside Hareshaw Burn near its confluence with the North Tyne. Bellingham has been a market town since the fifteenth century and a centre for North Tynedale industry. It has held regular cattle, sheep and wool fairs over the centuries and was also an important outlet for local craftsmen including cobblers, saddlers, tailors, blacksmiths and potters.

In 1162 North Tynedale passed into the custody of the Scots as recompense for the renunciation of inherited claims for the whole of Northumbria. It remained in Scottish hands until the mid fourteenth century. As a result of Northumberland's separation from the crown, the region was considered by the powers in London as an area best left to get on by itself. This outlook only served to increase the already bitter Border warfare and local family feuding.

The town's oldest building is St. Cuthbert's Church, dating back to the eleventh century. The thick stone walls, unusual barrel-vaulted stone roof and narrow windows bear testimony to the turbulent past. Such features would have helped provide a refuge for the locals and their livestock during border raids.

The building of the bridge in 1834 brought great rejoicing, as previously the river could only be crossed by a ford which had claimed many lives over the years. The picturesque four-arched bridge was designed by John Green, a favourite architect of the Duke of Northumberland. The old tollhouse is still in place at the southerly end of the bridge.

Among the medieval slabs in the graveyard is the 'Long Pack', its name derived from its unusual elongated narrow shape.

In 1732 a peddler called at Lee Hall, then the home of the Ridleys. The family were away at the time and a servant girl gave permission for the peddler to leave behind his pack of wares. Later the girl thought she saw the pack move and summoned help. A gun-bearing manservant fired at the suspicious bundle resulting in a loud scream and a copious flow of blood. On unwrapping the pack they discovered a body with a whistle around the neck. Neighbours were summoned and when darkness fell the whistle was blown. As suspected, a gang of robbers waiting for just such a signal attacked the Hall. They were mown down in a hail of bullets; the dead man inside the pack was never identified.

R. W. Thornton 2001

Hareshaw Linn

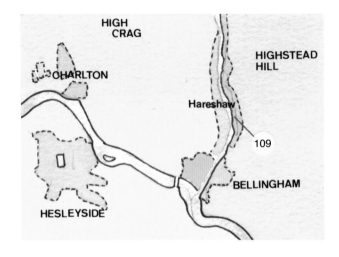

Hareshaw Burn - Bellingham

Hareshaw Linn is a pleasant mile-and-a-half's stroll from Bellingham through ancient deciduous woodland whose beauty is quite breathtaking. The area was very popular with the local residents, who used stones from the riverbed to lay the path that skirts the burn. They also built the seven rustic bridges that criss-cross the burn to bring visitors to the foot of what is widely acknowledged as one of the most beautiful waterfalls in Northumberland. Here the burn enters a deep, tree-shrouded thirty-foot cleft and in full spate, thunders down onto the sandstone river bed below.

It is difficult to imagine that this idyllic setting was once the heart of an industrial centre of some importance, Hareshaw Iron Works. The Duke of Northumberland had given approval for the mining of ironstone and coal from Hareshaw Common; as a result the ironworks were built in 1883 and duly leased to Messrs. Batson, Campion and Co. The works were substantial, consisting of two furnaces, later increased to three, a wagon way linking the works to the collieries and six rows of cottages to provide accommodation for some eighty workers and their families. The cottages were generously designed for the times, with a spacious living room, pantry and a loft as an additional sleeping area.

The venture met with little success, although it was reputed that some of the steel produced was used in the construction of the High Level Bridge. The reason for failure appeared to be the remote location, leading to high transportation and production costs. The basic cost of production was four pound per ton whilst the selling price was fixed at three pound per ton, leading to an unsustainable loss of some three hundred pound a week. In 1846 the works were declared bankrupt and taken over by the Union Bank of Newcastle before final closure in 1848.

All that now remains are traces of the wagon way, the dam and barely recognizable heaps of spoil.

R. W. Thornton 2001

Hesleyside Hall

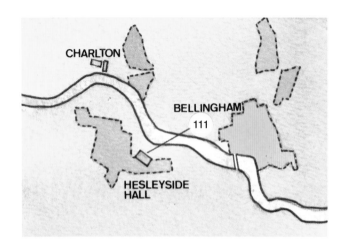

The Tower

Hesleyside Hall is a most imposing Georgian mansion on the southern bank of the River North Tyne, a mile west of Bellingham. It is surrounded by beautiful parklands and lawns that sweep down to the riverside. It has been the home of the Charlton family for centuries. The estate was laid out in 1776 by no less a person than Capability Brown and his admirable landscaping skills fittingly complement the fine architecture of the Hall. Of particular note is the handsome avenue of trees leading from the Hall to the river.

In 1783 the Hall suffered severe fire damage. During the lengthy period of restoration two further serious fires broke out. These events take on a chilling significance when we learn that the Hall had an ancient curse. Apparently in order to fulfil its destiny the home of the Charltons has to be burned down three times and then sink. The house sinking is a puzzle. It is possible that our ancestors may have had a premonition of the effects of global warming, so that the close proximity of the river may explain the mystery.

The Charltons are one of the oldest families in North Tynedale and at one time were the fiercest of the clans operating in the area, others being the Dodds, the Robsons and the Milburns. Throughout border history these names have echoed through Tynedale, striking terror into the hearts of law-abiding citizens. In the reign of Elizabeth I Sir Robert Bowes, a latter day trouble-shooter reported back on the lawless state of the border area and penned the following bleak missive to those in authority;

"The countrye of North Tyndail is more plenished with wild and misdeemed people, may make up of men on horsebak and upon foote about 600. They stand most by fower names, whereas Charltons be the chief."

A story goes that when the larder was bare the family matriarch would wait until the hungry men were sitting at the table and then arrive with a large dish. Their culinary expectations were dashed when she lifted the cover to reveal nothing more than a spur. Her message could not have been clearer; if you want something to eat, ride out and steal it!

R.W. Thornton 2001

Falstone

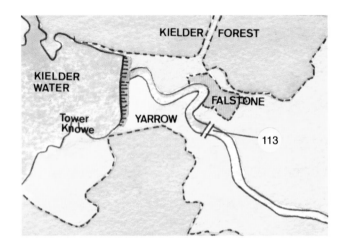

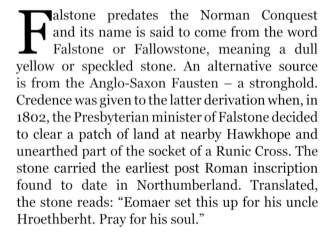

The Stone Bridge

Falstone predates the Norman Conquest and its name is said to come from the word Falstone or Fallowstone, meaning a dull yellow or speckled stone. An alternative source is from the Anglo-Saxon Fausten – a stronghold. Credence was given to the latter derivation when, in 1802, the Presbyterian minister of Falstone decided to clear a patch of land at nearby Hawkhope and unearthed part of the socket of a Runic Cross. The stone carried the earliest post Roman inscription found to date in Northumberland. Translated, the stone reads: "Eomaer set this up for his uncle Hroethberht. Pray for his soul."

Whatever the correct derivation, Falstone remains a pretty village eight miles north west of Bellingham on the banks of the North Tyne. It is surrounded by trees and unspoiled meadows, making a pleasant contrast with the bare fells and bleak moors in which it is set.

In earlier times the Robsons, a notorious Border clan, dominated the area. On one occasion they sallied forth bent on mischief into Liddesdale over the Scottish border. Their target was the Grahams, long-standing enemies. They stole or "shifted" a number of sheep, which proved to be diseased. On their return home the disease infected their own flocks. Intent on revenge they returned to Liddesdale and hanged seven of the Graham clan.

A rough risky place to dwell, Falstone was remote, hidden in a forest and on a road leading almost nowhere. It was largely a law unto itself. Controlling the local populace was no easy task and at times the Wardens must have despaired. Even the clergy struggled: the then Bishop of Durham commented that:

"...priests go with sword and dagger and in such coarse apparel as they can get."

Due to the remoteness of the area, Falstone was virtually self-sufficient with small-scale production of clothing, farm tools, iron and tin ware while numerous small coalmines were worked in the area. The mine at nearby Shillburnhaugh was said to produce the best coal in Northumberland and the second best in England!

Before the bridge was built in 1843, the only means of crossing the river was by a hazardous ford. Sir John Swinburne built the stone-built three-arched bridge, largely at his own expense. The rail line up the North Tyne Valley opened in 1861 and played a significant role in opening up the district to trade and farming.

Falstone is now in the heart of walking country next to Kielder Reservoir and has become a centre for tourism.

R.W. Thornton 2002

Kielder

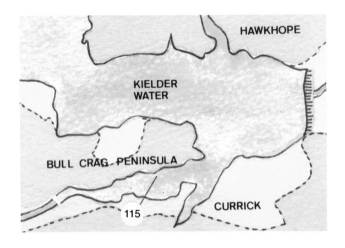

Presbyterian Church

"In the year it appears that the lands in North Tynedale were a great forest full of woods and deer."

This is how those lands were described in a 1750 report on the Duke of Northumberland's estates.

Very little of this ancient forest was left by the early nineteenth century, as an increasing population and associated industrial growth brought great demand for timber for housing, flooring, furniture, pit props and coal staithes. Mid-Victorian landowners saw this gap between supply and demand and decided that commercial forestry was a winner.

Early attempts at tree planting met with little success. The area was high and exposed, the lack of relevant knowledge and experience led to failure. In 1927, the Forestry Commission acquired land, including Kielder Castle from the Duke of Northumberland in lieu of death duties. It promptly planted forty-five acres of mixed conifer; Norwegian spruce, Sitka spruce, Scots pine and Japanese larch. This was the beginning of the largest man-made forest in Europe, which eventually covered two hundred and thirty square miles containing around one hundred and twenty million trees. It also brought much-needed employment to this remote area, leading in turn to good quality housing and schools. Early forestry work involved a great deal of hard manual labour entailing a five-and-a-half-day week toiling in all weathers. Technological advances later streamlined the industry and the workforce was dramatically cut.

Kielder Forest did not meet with universal approval. The planting of trees on such a scale profoundly altered the landscape of Tynedale; many thought that the mass of trees obstructed and blurred the dramatic skyline of the rolling hills. Certainly little thought had been given to aesthetic considerations; priority was given to the mass production of timber. Public relations were further strained when stringent laws were enforced to keep walkers away. The area is now much more user-friendly. Indeed it is now arguably Northumberland's greatest single tourist destination, attracting over three hundred thousand visitors every year.

The Duke of Northumberland decided to build a castle at Kielder above the confluence of the Kielder Burn and the North Tyne. The foundations were laid in 1772 and the building completed in 1775. The castle was built around a courtyard, approached by an arched entrance. The main building had battlements and Gothic windows and was used as a shooting lodge until acquired by the Forestry Commission. It now serves as an information and exhibition centre.

R. W. THORNTON 2002

Kielder Water

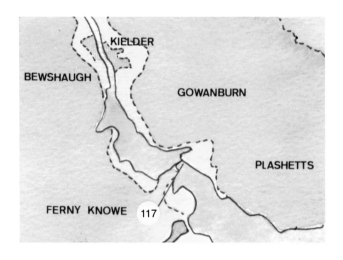

Kielder Dam

It is impossible now to imagine what Kielder looked like before the "Water" was created. In the early 1970's, predictions suggested that demand for water from the industrial Tyne, Tees and Wear areas would soon exceed supply. This led to several sites for a new reservoir being explored. Kielder seemed the only one capable of meeting estimated demands. It also appeared to involve the least environmental and social upheaval because relatively few dwellings would be submerged and the dominance of the great conifer forest limited the area's natural beauty. Nevertheless, the scheme still proved highly controversial.

After prolonged wrangling, Parliament approved the Kielder Water Scheme in 1974. To re-house those directly affected, twenty-six new houses were built at Bellingham and Falstone.

Northumbrian Water undertook the project, with support from other water authorities. It created the largest man-made reservoir in Europe, which was opened by the Queen in 1982. It is seven miles long; the enormous amount of water it holds is illustrated by the fact that if every person in the world flushed a toilet simultaneously, even that sudden demand could be met.

Bakethin Reservoir is five miles from the main dam and acts as an amenity dam to hold water used to cover any unsightly mudflats otherwise exposed in the main reservoir when large amounts of water are released. The area around it is a designated nature reserve, which has proved a notable success. The fact that the water level remains constant encourages a wide variety of flora and fauna to flourish.

Although the industrial demand for water has not been as great as anticipated, Kielder Water is undoubtedly a marvellous technical achievement. Its expanse has great aesthetic appeal, and supports many leisure activities including; sailing, camping and fishing. A salmon hatchery was built to compensate for lost spawning grounds above the weirs. As a result, huge numbers of young salmon are released into the North Tyne to return – if they are lucky – as adults. It has also assisted the environmental re-birth of the River Tyne.

R.W. THORNTON 2002

Kielder Viaduct

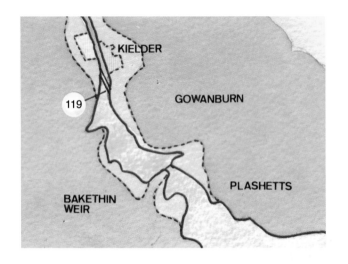

Kielder Viaduct

In 1854 the first turf was cut at Tyne Green, Hexham by William Henry Charlton to herald the construction of a single rail track leading up the North Tyne Valley as far as Plashetts colliery at Belling Burn. Later the line was extended to link up with the Carlisle to Edinburgh line at Riccarts over the Scottish Border.

The North Tyne was crossed near Kielder Castle by a seven-arched viaduct. The chosen crossing point meant that the viaduct had to be built at an angle with the line of the river that resulted in arch building of tremendous complexity. One can only admire the skill of Peter Nicholson. He calculated the individual shape of each stone used to make a perfect fit – a notable achievement.

With the viaduct in sight of Kielder Castle, approval for the design had to be given consideration by the then Duke of Northumberland. He insisted the structure be in the appropriate castellated style with turrets and battlements, no less than thirty-two crenellations along each side. The construction of the railway and viaduct – between 1885 and 1862 saw a large influx of rail navvies moving into this remote area: Irish, Scottish and English, many brought large families.

The railway was not a success. The coal mined at Plashetts proved to be unsuitable for local industry and another important customer, Hareshaw Iron Works, closed down shortly after the line opened. There were very few passengers and as a result only three trains, each with a single carriage, ran every day.

Inevitably the line closed; first the passenger service in 1956, then the freight line two years later. The Kielder Viaduct became the property of the Forestry Commission, who in turn sold it to the Northumberland and Newcastle Society. The viaduct had been listed as a Historic Building and so funding was made available for restoration. This entailed replacing defective stonework, re-pointing the arches and resurfacing and waterproofing the carriageway, while the base of the piers was encased in a grit-blasted concrete skin. Kielder Viaduct is now preserved as an outstanding example of Victorian railway architecture.

R.W. Thornton 2002

North Tyne Source

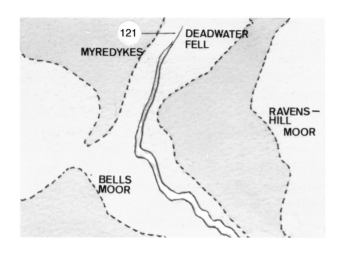

Kerseycleugh Bridge

To trace the source of the North Tyne it is necessary to travel beyond Kielder to the western limits of the Cheviot Hills to Peel Fell. At nearly two thousand feet above sea level on the Scottish/English border, on a clear day the summit offers breath-taking views in all directions. From here both the west and east coasts can be seen, as can Cross Fell, the source of the South Tyne. Swinburne, in his "Jacobean Exile" captures the mood superbly;

"On Kielderside the wind blows wide

There sounds nae hunting horn

That rings sae sweet as the winds that beat

Round the banks where Tyne is born."

On the lower slopes of Peel Fell lies the level-plain known as Deadwater Fell. This acid, peaty soil restricts vegetation growth to heather and a tussocky grass known locally as, "Scotsmen's Heads". It is claimed that here, at Deadwater, lies the true source of the North Tyne, a matter of only a few metres inside the English side of the border. Here it seeps through the coarse grass often appearing motionless, as if pondering on its final destination – hence Deadwater. It is difficult to appreciate that from such a humble, faltering beginning; the Tyne will eventually develop into one of the world's most famous rivers.

There are claims that a "sulphur well" once existed in the area. In the eighteenth century people suffering from skin ailments travelled many miles in hope of a cure. There were a number of wooden huts for bathing purposes but no remains of them have ever been found; a pity – "Deadwater Spa" would have had a ring to it.

The Kielder Stone, an enormous flat-topped boulder is a landmark. It lies at the head of Scaup Burn and is said to have acted as a post box during the many years of border skirmishes. Clan members of either side left letters in niches for collection as they passed by, perhaps they found their destination, and such trust deserves success.

The Victorian railway that served the region is long gone. Deadwater Railway Station sat on each side of the border and must surely have served one of the most thinly populated areas in the country. Trains only stopped here three times a week. The building still exists and is now a private dwelling.

R.W. Thornton 2002

The South Tyne

I cannot get tae my love if I would dee
For the waters of the Tyne run between him and me
And here I maun stand wi a tear in my ee
All sighin and sobbin, my true love to see

Oh where is the boatman, my bonny hinney
Oh where is the boatman, go bring him to me
For to ferry me over the Tyne to my honey
Or speed him across the rough waters to me

Oh bring me a boatman, I'll gi all my money
And you for your trouble rewarded shall be
If you'll carry me over the Tyne to my honey
And I will remember the boatman and thee

I cannot get tae my love if I would dee
For the waters of the Tyne run between him and me
And here I maun stand wi a tear in my ee
All sighin and sobbin, my true love to see

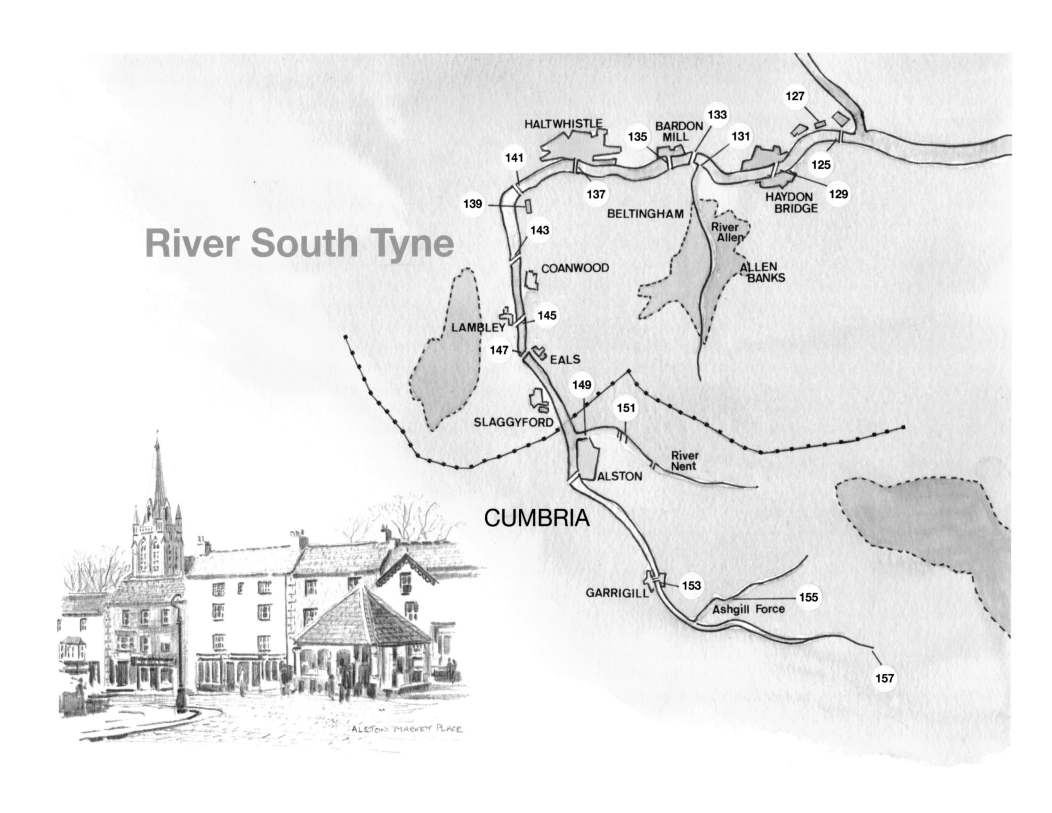

River South Tyne

127

HALTWHISTLE
135 BARDON MILL 133
141 131
137
139
143
BELTINGHAM
125
HAYDON BRIDGE
129
River Allen
ALLEN BANKS
COANWOOD
145
LAMBLEY
147 EALS
149
SLAGGYFORD
151
River Nent
ALSTON

CUMBRIA

GARRIGILL 153
155
Ashgill Force
157

ALSTON MARKET PLACE

Warden

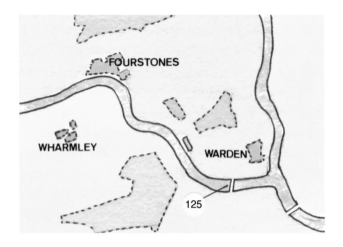

Boathouse Inn

Warden is a hamlet two miles north west of Hexham in the angle of land formed where the rivers North and South Tyne join. During the reign of Edward III, Warden was part of the Priory lands of Hexham, extending to just over twenty acres of land with six cottages, a ferry and a manor house.

Beyond the village stands the prominent Warden Hill where the outline of a Celtic fort can still be seen complete with protective stone walls. The fort was later occupied by the Romans and then by the invading Saxons, who drove the Britons out. They cleared the trees and built a settlement on the riverbanks, retaining the ancient fort as a lookout post, named it 'Weard Dunn' from which Warden is derived.

Until the nineteenth century the only direct access to Warden from the south side of the river was by ford. The ford to the east was known as 'High Ford' and was used by coal miners on route to the colliery at Acomb. Later on a ferry service, "The West Boat" operated between the Hexham and the Boatside Inn, which is another venue with a claim to be the origin of the Northumberland folk song "The Water of Tyne".

The ferry was superseded by an elegant suspension bridge opened in 1826. It was rebuilt after collapsing under the weight of a thresher. This bridge was eventually replaced in 1903 by the present two-arched stone bridge. The old tollhouse remains at the south end.

Of particular interest in Warden is The Church of St Michael and All Angels; people have worshipped here for over fourteen hundred years. It has a fine Saxon tower built mainly of Roman stone. The upper section was badly damaged by fire, possibly by beacons lit from the inside to warn of impending raids. It was restored in 1765. An early seventh-century cross can be found at the entrance and a collection of small Saxon coffins and grave covers is on display in the porch.

In nearby Homer's Lane lived Joseph Hedley, a well-known and well-liked character who made highly sought-after quilts. After his cottage remained closed for several days, locals broke open the door and found that Joe had been brutally murdered. Despite a reward of £100, a great deal of money at the time, the murderer was never found.

R.W. Thornton 2001

Fourstones Paper Mill

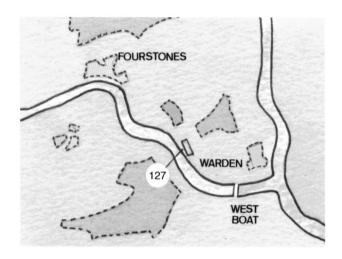

Fourstones Paper Mill from the A69

The South Tyne Paper Mill was the first paper mill in Northumberland, founded in 1763. At first the paper was made by hand, a laborious process where the best quality paper was made from rope and inferior papers were produced from the pulp of old tarpaulins and other rags that came to hand. Around the mid-nineteenth century, hand mills began to experience competition from papermaking machines and in the 1840's the mill management installed a machine.

The name of the factory was changed to the Warden Paper Mill in the 1860s and the mill started to import esparto grass as an alternative to rag pulp; about sixty people were employed. In 1907 the name was changed to the Fourstones Paper Mill and has over the years returned to using rag pulp. During the 1960's the mill diversified into a new product; cellulose wadding for use in hospitals. Today Fourstones Paper Mill can be justifiably proud of the fact that it is one of the oldest paper mills in the country still in production.

R.W. THORNTON 2001

Haydon Bridge

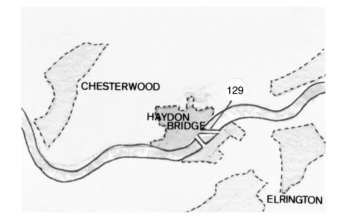

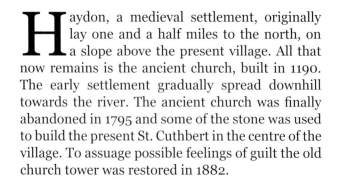

The Concrete Bridge

Haydon, a medieval settlement, originally lay one and a half miles to the north, on a slope above the present village. All that now remains is the ancient church, built in 1190. The early settlement gradually spread downhill towards the river. The ancient church was finally abandoned in 1795 and some of the stone was used to build the present St. Cuthbert in the centre of the village. To assuage possible feelings of guilt the old church tower was restored in 1882.

A wooden bridge was first recorded in 1309 and was gated to keep out unwelcome visitors when beacons signalled an imminent raid. Lawlessness was so prevalent in the South Tyne Valley that an order was issued in 1553 directing watches to be kept under the control of the regional Wardens. Local inhabitants were allocated to guard vulnerable areas throughout the night, usually two men to each location. It is on record that two of the Wardens, belonging to the Ridley and Heron clans, were openly accused of secretly siding with the Scottish invaders during a particularly violent raid on Haydon Bridge.

Haydon Bridge is famous for its school, The Shaftoe Trust Grammar School, founded in 1658 by the Rev. John Shaftoe of the "Bobby Shaftoe" legend. Here any boy or girl within the parish could claim free education. Subjects on offer were; English grammar, writing, geography, mathematics and the art of navigation. For an additional penny per term, instruction in Latin and Greek were also available. This must speak volumes for the pedigree of the staff at the time.

The laudable intention of offering free education to such a high standard was not wholly appreciated by the local community. They thought the process "high-minded" and offering little to equip the pupils for the practical needs of local employment. The inclusion of navigation may have had some bearing on their outlook.

John Martin, a pupil of the above school, was one of a family of thirteen children born in a small cottage at Land's End Farm in 1789. He rose from humble beginnings to become an internationally recognized artist. He painted mainly biblical scenes, often of apocalyptic visions and possibly using the local landscape as background. These skilfully - executed oil paintings took fashionable London by storm. He later wrote, with a hint of bitterness: "By birth my station could scarcely have been humbler than it was. My father's disposition kept the family exceedingly poor..."

Two brothers were also to achieve renown of sorts, one for setting fire to York Minster and another for his ability to play the violin walking backwards.

The original stone bridge built in the late seventeenth century was destroyed by the Great Flood of 1771. The replacement bridge was built in 1774 but has suffered extensive damage over several centuries. In 1967 a temporary steel bridge was added, later modified and re-erected at Corbridge. The old bridge was restored, pedestrianised and in 1970, scheduled as an Ancient Monument.

R.W. Thornton 2001

River Allen

Allenheads

The River Allen is formed from two rivers, the East and West Allens. They both rise in on bleak moor land, rich in minerals and fed by innumerable peaty burns. They continue their separate ways for eleven and a half miles before uniting near the Cupola Bridge to form the River Allen, where it continues for a further four miles before joining the South Tyne.

The Cupola Bridge derives its name from a bygone lead smelter that operated in the immediate neighbourhood and which had been authorized by an Act Of Parliament in 1778. The bridge, a handsome structure of three arches, was hugely instrumental in the development of the local lead industry. It is a gentle prelude to a series of taxing hairpin bends that carry the road up a steep, rocky face. The summit reveals splendid views over the deep ravine at Staward, through which the Allen tumbles over its rocky bed. Trees of numerous varieties cling to the precipitous banks that are overlooked by the ruins of Staward Pele.

The pele, a ruined tower incorporating a large number of Roman stones, was in the possession of the friars of Hexham during the fourteenth century; beneath it lies Cyper's Linn, a dark, sombre pool said to be bottomless. It is also said that the friars had warning of an impending raid and rather than relinquish their gold and precious possessions they packed them into a chest and lowered them into the pool. Many years after, an optimistic local farmer set out to retrieve the sunken treasure but while trying to haul the chest from the water, the poor beasts and their owner were dragged into the pool and never seen again.

Allen is a Celtic word meaning, "silver shining." The Allendale area certainly shone in terms of mineral deposits and during the seventeenth and eighteenth centuries the area became the largest producer of lead in the world. At one time there were over thirty mines and mills within the Dales. The Blacketts and the Beaumonts, who owned a great deal of the land, acquired the mineral rights. The industry declined in the face of increasing overseas competition and by the end of the nineteenth century had virtually ceased production.

Ridley Bridge

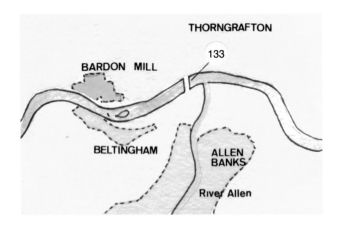

Ridley Hall

Travelling west along the A69 beyond Haydon Bridge, a road-sign points left to Ridley and Beltingham. A steep downhill road then leads towards Ridley Bridge, which spans the River South Tyne en route to the magnificent Ridley Hall. The Georgian bridge is a handsome affair with two stone arches, built in 1792 and designed by J. Mylne who also created the Georgian Tyne Bridge. The bridge was built to link Ridley Hall with the main east-west highway, as the existing roads and incline at the time were too steep for horse and carriage.

This is Ridley country - once the territory of this most feared and powerful clan whose first recorded appearance in Northumberland dates back to the twelfth century. Ridley Hall was first mentioned in 1567 as property held by the Ridleys and it is possible that at one time a fortified house existed as the family seat. The Lowes family acquired the property in the latter part of the seventeenth century and William Lowes built an impressive mansion overlooking the River Allen.

The Hall and estates passed into the hands of the Bowes-Lyon family and in 1891, the Hall after falling into disrepair was rebuilt in lavish neo-Tudor style. When the Hon. Francis Bowes-Lyon died in 1947, the property was sold; the farmland to the Catholic Trust, the Hall and remaining estate to the Rev. E. A. Evans who used it to re-house his boys' preparatory school based in Hexham. Today the building is used by Northumberland County Council as a residential education centre.

Close to Ridley Hall lies the picturesque hamlet of Beltingham lying in the crook of land formed by the River Allen and the River South Tyne. Its mellow, stone-roofed cottages and ancient church, encircling a small village green presents a delightful landscape of rural tranquillity. The church dates from the sixteenth Century and is dedicated to St. Cuthbert. It is suggested that his remains were laid here on their journey to Durham when the monks of Lindisfarne fled their Viking invaders. In the churchyard there is a yew tree whose gnarled trunk is encircled by two bands of metal for support. It is almost nine hundred years old and still flourishing! The tree would almost certainly have been used to make long bows in past turbulent times. It is also highly probable that the most famous of the Ridleys, Nicholas, Bishop of London, once of Willimoteswick Castle, was baptised in and attended St. Cuthbert's as a child. On the accession of Mary Tudor he was faced with the stark choice of renouncing his faith or losing his life. He chose the latter and was burned at the stake in October 1555 at Oxford alongside Bishop Latimer. Who cannot be moved by the words of comfort offered by Latimer as the flames rose.

"Be of good comfort, Master Ridley, and play the man. We shall this day light a candle, by God's grace, in England, as I trust shall never be put out."

R.W. Thornton 2001

Bardon Mill

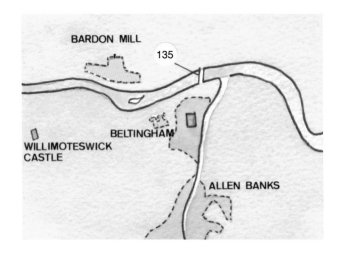

Willimoteswick Castle

Bardon Mill is a small hamlet on the north bank of the River South Tyne, five miles east of Haltwhistle. It is suggested that the name is derived from the woollen mills that operated in the late seventeenth century. The mills were water-powered and produced baize cloth. An alternative explanation is that the name comes from a Barron or Burrow situated on a hill overlooking the area.

Wool production was not the only industry that encroached upon this beautiful stretch of the South Tyne Valley. For centuries coal had been worked in the area. Bardon Mill Colliery, a drift mine opened by local businessman J. Pepperell, bordered the Military Road. Under nationalisation the work force peaked at three hundred and twenty. The roof was likened to a giant sponge, from which water constantly seeped into the workings requiring constant pumping day and night. The mine eventually closed in 1973.

The Bardon Mill pottery was established in 1878 in what used to be an old woollen mill and has been central to life in the village. It is still in business today and exports high quality products to a worldwide market.

The Millhouse Ford was the only means of crossing the river in early days. In 1542 Henry VIII, exasperated beyond measure at the scale of reiving, commanded that two local men guard the ford every night in an attempt to alleviate the problem. The river had a propensity for sudden and dramatic flooding, so the use of the ford was at times hazardous. In 1883 a much-needed footbridge was paid for by public subscription: the iron footbridge known as the Millhouse Bridge, was just over thirty eight yards in length and built along the alignment of the ford, just east of the railway station.

Willimoteswick Castle, a former border stronghold, stands on a small knoll across the river. Its history is obscure but it is thought to have been built in the twelfth/thirteenth centuries. The castle was the principal seat of the ancient Ridley family and is generally accepted as the birthplace of the protestant martyr Bishop Nicholas Ridley. Today the ruins are incorporated in a farmhouse, the magnificent tower acting as the only entrance to the building.

R.W. Thornton 2001

Haltwhistle

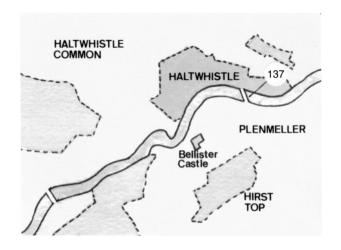

Bellister Castle

Haltwhistle is a market town licensed by King John in 1207. There is a false supposition that the name is derived from the railway. In fact, the likely origin is hautwessel or hautwysel meaning "watch on the high mound" or possibly haltwysel, for "a meeting of streams by the hill", as there is a burn that runs into the Tyne.

During more than three hundred years of constant Border feuding, Haltwhistle probably suffered more than most. Robbery, murder, kidnap and arson were common occurrences. This is evident by the remains of a large number of fortified dwellings in the area; Haltwhistle has more defensible houses than any other English town. At one time there were two pele towers, one of which can still be seen incorporated into the Red Lion Hotel. The other, believed at one time to be Haltwhistle's main defence, was Musgrove Tower (1415), which enjoyed a commanding position on Castle Hill. Unfortunately this was demolished in 1963, - a sorry indictment of bureaucratic insensitivity to history.

Gradually life became more peaceful and the town's first school opened in 1719. Slowly industry developed, giving rise to woollen mills, grain mills and a brewery. Progress escalated dramatically with the arrival of the railway in 1883; at last full advantage could be taken of the rich mineral fields in the area, in particular coal and lead. In 1846 an act was passed to build a branch line to Alston. The viaduct, opened in 1851 to carry the line across the river, is no longer in use but still dominates the area.

Bellister Castle is well known locally for its ghost, there are various versions of the story but the gist of the tale is this. A wandering minstrel seeking shelter for the night was welcomed into the castle by Lord Bellister. As the evening progressed, Lord Bellister became suspicious, he developed a level of paranoia and took the view that his guest was a spy sent by his enemies. The minstrel detected the change in atmosphere, felt uneasy and decided to sneak away. As far his Lordship was concerned, this only confirmed his suspicions, he set his bloodhounds off in pursuit. The luckless minstrel was torn to pieces on the river bank and his ghost, "The Grey Man of Bellister" is believed to haunt the grounds, castle and surrounding area.

R.W. Thornton 2001

Featherstone Castle

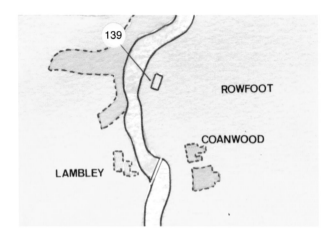

Featherstone Castle

Situated four miles south west of Haltwhistle on the banks of the River South Tyne, Featherstone is regarded as one of the most impressive castles in Northumberland. Nearby are the hamlets of Park Village and Rowfoot, each consisting mainly of eighteenth and nineteenth-century cottages. Rowfoot was the site of the late Featherstone Park Railway Station until the line was axed in 1976. The old school is now the village hall; the Wallace Arms still offers warm hospitality.

Prior to the thirteenth century the site contained a fortified house built of stone, a rarity in those days. The first recorded owner was Helias de Featherstonehaugh in 1212. Over the centuries as the building gradually developed, a strong L-shaped tower was added for further protection. In the seventeenth century, the two buildings were joined by a manor house; this is now the west front housing the main entrance. Following the Civil War the castle and estates were confiscated by the Crown, as the Featherstones were Roman Catholics and considered to be on the "wrong side." Eventually the estate was bought back by a Featherstone who happened to be Protestant and sold on to James Wallace, a future Attorney General, in the middle of the eighteenth century. His son Thomas accrued sufficient wealth through various Admiralty and government positions for extensive development of the castle and estate.

By all accounts the Featherstonehaughs were a violent breed, deeply involved in both local and national conflicts. Their bitterest enemies were the local Ridley clan from nearby Willimoteswick. In 1530 Sir Albany Featherstonehaugh had the misfortune to be hacked to death less than a mile from his own castle by a band of marauders apparently containing a number of Ridleys. It not surprising to learn that the leader of the group, William Ridley was himself murdered by the Featherstonehaughs shortly after.

Not suprisingly the castle has its ghosts. The story unfolds with Abigail Featherstonehaugh falling in love with one Dick Ridley, human nature being what it is! Her outraged father made it very clear that she was not going to marry a Ridley and to make doubly sure married her off to Thomas Blenkinsopp very much against her will. After the wedding ceremony at Haltwhistle the wedding party, as was the custom, rode out to "beat the bounds" and were ambushed by a lurking band of Ridleys led by the devastated Dick. During the bloody skirmish, Abigail bravely placed herself between her new husband and her erstwhile lover to prevent further mischief and was accidentally killed. Overcome by remorse, Dick Ridley promptly took his own life. It is reputed that the rest of the wedding party, anxiously waiting at the castle for the return of the long overdue group were relieved to hear the clatter of horses' hoofs. But when the main hall door swung open the dead who included the groom, entered in a ghostly procession carrying their heads. At the sight of it, Abigail's father fell down dead with shock. Legend has it that as darkness falls on each anniversary the wedding couple can be seen riding through the woods.

R.W. THORNTON 2001

Featherstone Bridge

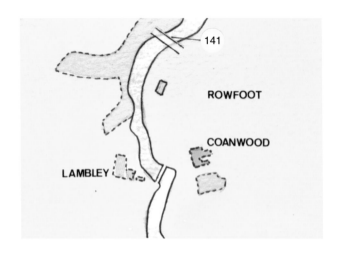

Featherstone Bridge

Featherstone Bridge is one of only two pre-nineteenth century bridges to cross the River South Tyne; the other is at Eals. It was built in 1778 close to the haughs of Featherstone Castle with a high stone-built arch to counter the effects of flooding. It is striking in that the keystone and the peak of the arch are out of alignment. This gives the bridge a rather unusual lopsided appearance.

Featherstone Bridge played a significant role in the industrial development of the South Tyne Valley. The crossing here was vitally important as it allowed lead ore to be transported from the Alston district to the smelting works at Haltwhistle.

Not far from the bridge, Pynkinscleugh Burn joins the River South Tyne, where until quite recently were the ruins of a small stone cottage, once the home of an eccentric old woman called Pearson.

She was blessed with a rather long, grey beard and went under the unfortunate soubriquet of "Beardy Grey." Reputed to be a prophetess, she claimed to tell the future, no doubt living on the credulity of her superstitious neighbours. Many of her utterances were passed down from parents to children and some are still remembered today. Pearson, would sit on a large stone outside her cottage on the banks of the river at midnight, where she would communicate with unknown forces in an attempt to reveal the future. One dark, stormy night she disappeared, never to be seen again. Her neighbours thought evil spirits had claimed her; it is more likely she was swept away by the river.

One of her recorded prophecies makes chilling reading. She claimed that if the lintel stone above her cottage door were ever removed, "Rivers of blood would flow." In fact estate workers removed the lintel from the ruins in 1914 and for the next four years the First World War raged. Indeed rivers of blood did run as never before! Pearson also warned that if the large rock she sat upon, should ever be covered in moss, a great battle would take place at Featherstone involving great loss of life. Many years after her disappearance it was noticed that the stone was very nearly covered. Locals broke the rock into small pieces and scattered them widely. It appears to have worked!

It was near Pynkinscleugh Burn that the Featherstone wedding massacre took place. For some time after the incident, local anglers claimed that the trout caught here were the finest-tasting in the area due to the blood that had been spilled in the river.

Coanwood

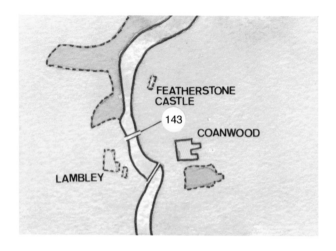

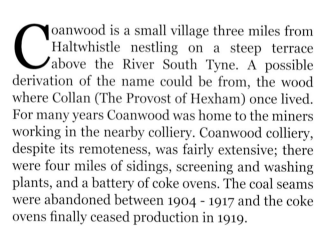

The Cupola Bridge - Whitfield

Coanwood is a small village three miles from Haltwhistle nestling on a steep terrace above the River South Tyne. A possible derivation of the name could be from, the wood where Collan (The Provost of Hexham) once lived. For many years Coanwood was home to the miners working in the nearby colliery. Coanwood colliery, despite its remoteness, was fairly extensive; there were four miles of sidings, screening and washing plants, and a battery of coke ovens. The coal seams were abandoned between 1904 - 1917 and the coke ovens finally ceased production in 1919.

The village was once a bustling, if small, community. A meeting house belonging to the Society of Friends was built in 1760 and in 1883 a Wesleyan Chapel was added. For many years a pub, The Sportsman's Arms, nicknamed the "Jerry," served not only Coanwood but also many outlying villages and hamlets. It was strictly a beer house, no spirits were served. The jugs and glasses were filled directly from the barrels in the cellar and laboriously carried up into the bar. Women were not allowed on the premises! Some tipplers, after a night of merriment, often staggered home during many a pitch black night via Lambley Viaduct; a strictly illegal and highly dangerous practice.

The school took in scholars from a wide area although the journey in the winter months must have been horrendous. Roads throughout the district were of a low standard and were often the cause of great hardship in winter when the regular horses and traps carrying much needed supplies, were unable to get through. There are people who still remember walking through snowdrifts down to Haltwhistle to carry back food and provisions in pillowcases. Many people kept hens and a pig or two.

Because of the remoteness "Tommy Shops" were set up in the area by colliery owners and railway contractors as a source of provision for their workers. Unfortunately they were often subject to abuse. Poor quality products and foodstuff were bought in cheaply and sold on at high prices. The hapless customers, having nowhere else to go, had little choice but to purchase the shoddy goods. This situation gave rise to the well-known saying, "A load of tommy rot!"

Because of the poor road network in the area, the decision to close the Haltwhistle – Alston branch line was opposed by the inhabitants of the valley. After a great deal of arguing the final decision to close the line was taken in January 1973, but only after agreement had been reached to provide an "all-weather road" to link the area effectively with Haltwhistle. The Diamond Oak Bridge, depicted in the painting, is an intrinsic part of the road system. The very first snows of winter, following the closure of the railway line, blocked the much-vaunted all-weather road.

Lambley Viaduct

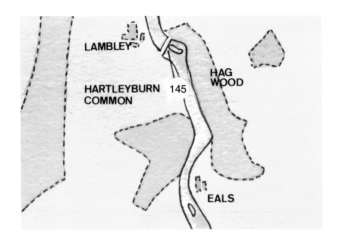

Lambley Railway Station

Lambley village was once a thriving community, housing miners who worked for a small local colliery. A hundred years ago it supported a confectioners, post office, butcher and resident doctor. The colliery closed in the 1950s and the population has dwindled. Today its famous viaduct overshadows the village.

In 1839, Newcastle and Carlisle were linked by rail through a relatively easy route along the South Tyne Valley. By 1862 Alston beckoned, offering lead, silver and limestone freight as a tantalizing reward. However installing the thirteen-mile line to Alston would not be easy, requiring a number of viaducts to span the steep-sided valley.

The largest of these viaducts was to be the Lambley Viaduct, designed by Sir George Barclay Bruce. The attractiveness of the design was further enhanced by the glorious wooded surroundings. Autumn was a special time to travel; trains would slow down to enable passengers to photograph the spectacle.

There is very little information about the work force that built the viaduct. Apparently the majority was from either Ireland or Scotland, some were lodged in the few local houses whilst the majority lived in a "camp" near Slaggyford.

The line closed in 1976 and the viaduct rapidly deteriorated. Masonry began to flake away, rendering the footbridge below unsafe. This was a wooden bridge built at the foot of the arches to enable residents from across the river gain access to the station. Scots pine and birch tree seedlings sprouted from the deck and the facing masonry, while vandals aided the process of decay. Extensive restoration work took place including the building of a new footbridge below the viaduct a few yards downstream. Now owned by the South Tyne Heritage Trust. It is open to pedestrians and is now an important part of the South Tyne Trail.

R.W. Thornton '2001

Eals

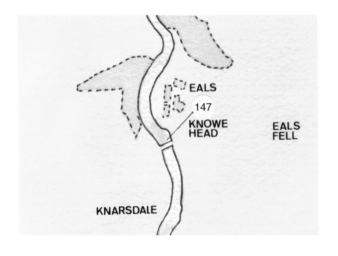

Eals Methodist Chapel

Tucked away off the beaten track is Eals, a straggling ribbon of cottages and farmhouses on the bank of the River South Tyne six miles west of Haltwhistle. This early settlement was different from any other in the immediate area in that it followed the Cumbrian style of farming based on the strip method. Each farmer had three strips of land to plough, three strips for meadow and a single, larger strip on higher land for grazing "up-top". It is possible to observe the distinctive patterns of the unusual layout in the dry stone-wall enclosures.

The flow of the river used to be irregular and was prone to flood resulting in a series of temporary islands created from river debris, hence the name Eals (Isles). Early settlers created farmland by building stone embankments to contain the river course.

At the east end of the hamlet a ford used to cross the river. This was well known to Moss-troopers and others bent on mischief in the time of the border raids. As a result a rota was drawn up detailing two men to guard the ford every night. Today a modern steel footbridge has replaced the ford.

The Eals Bridge built in 1733 links the hamlet to the Knarsdale parish. It is a fine-stone-built structure with two high segmental arches designed to avoid flood damage. The nearby pub, The Kirkside Inn, was formerly the home of the resident minister of St Judes parish church that was built in 1883 to replace a much older building on the same site. Knarsdale Hall, a handsome seventeenth-century fortified farm is built on a prominence, which may have been a Norman motte and bailey castle. It dominates the area and naturally has a ghost story. Apparently at one time an elderly man lived in Knarsdale Hall with his niece and nephew. The elderly man married a much younger woman who then fell for the charms of the nephew. The couple knew that the niece strongly disapproved and plotted her demise. One dark, stormy night they lured her to a local pond and drowned her. Later they were confronted by her dripping wet ghost causing the nephew to flee, never to return whilst his lover became totally deranged.

R.W. Thornton 2001

Alston

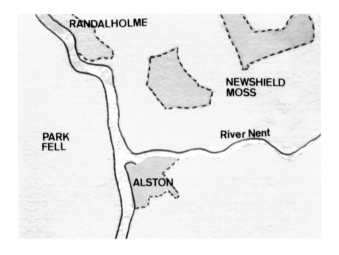

The Market Square

Alston dates back to the twelfth century when it was known as Aldenby. The Romans are known to have mined for lead in the area. In the early seventeenth century, when Sir Francis Radcliffe's family bought the local manor, the vast lead reserves were exploited and the town of Alston developed. By 1673 there were one hundred and nineteen mines within the parish and by the nineteenth century annual production was eight thousand tons. Many churches and great buildings throughout Europe were roofed with Alston lead. Silver, copper, iron and limestone were also mined. If it were not for the remains of the workings, it would be difficult to believe that the town was a major industrial centre.

The mines are now gone; Alston is a popular, attractive town now more geared towards the ever-expanding tourist trade. Built into a hillside, its quaint, cobbled main street slopes steeply down towards the River South Tyne. It is a town of character and history. Over the years it has vied with Buxton in the Peak district as the highest market town in England. Sadly Alston no longer has a market but retains its distinctive market cross erected in 1764 with money given by Sir William Stephenson who, at the time, was the Lord Mayor of London and was born in Alston parish. Over the years the cross has suffered wear and tear – notably in more recent times from motor vehicles unable to negotiate the steep, cobbled street. It has always been meticulously restored, a testimony to local pride.

Many stone buildings date back to the seventeenth and eighteenth centuries while the church contains a clock from Dilston Hall, obtained when the estate was forfeited to the Crown following the Radcliffes' disastrous involvement in the Jacobite Rebellion.

The rail branch line from Haltwhistle to Alston opened in 1852, bringing increased prosperity to the town. The line was due for closure in the 1960s, courtesy of Dr. Beeching, but vigorous local opposition delayed the closure until 1972. The following year the South Tynedale Railway Preservation Society was formed. In 1984 it opened up a narrow-gauge line using part of the old track. Over the years the project has continued to develop into an important and extremely popular tourist attraction.

R. W. THORNTON 2002

The Gossips - River Nent

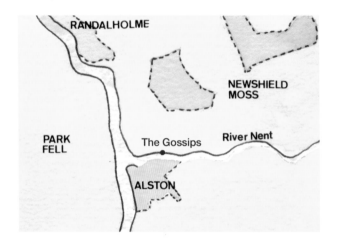

Riverside Walk

The Nent is shorter and narrower but significantly deeper than its neighbouring burns and so enjoys the distinction of being classed as a river. Its source, at Nenthead on the Alston Moor, has a durable and eminent history of lead mining dating back to Roman times. It is believed that German miners worked the area during medieval times, although it was not until the eighteenth century, with significant expansion and development of the lead trade, that the area flourished.

The lead ore produced in the area contained an unusually high quantity of silver, estimated at 1134 grams per ton of lead, which was extracted during the smelting process. Such a windfall did not escape the attention of Henry I who ordered that all silver recovered should be claimed by the Crown and handed over to the Carlisle Mint. During the ensuing years, lead miners working the Alston Moors enjoyed "Royal Protection" to ensure continued output of silver.

The Quaker-owned London Lead Company built a village at Nenthead in 1753 to house their workers and families. Their mines would exploit the rich deposits of lead ore found close by. Most unusually for the times, the new owners insisted on high standards of welfare. Cottages replaced old huts; a school, a library and a chapel were built and medical services were provided to support and sustain the labour force.

In 1776 the Company commissioned the engineer, John Smeaton, (who was later to rebuild the Eddystone lighthouse) along with Joseph Walton, to build an underground navigable canal between Nenthead and Alston. This was to be five miles long and lined with stone. Its purpose was to help drain the Nenthead mines, explore for new mineral veins and provide a possible means of transport. Building progress proved to be slow and expensive and in 1817 mounting costs forced the project to be abandoned. The section of the canal, which had been completed however apparently, became very

popular in Victorian times. Boats, complete with guides, could be hired for romantic underground canal voyages with flickering torchlight and musical accompaniment. The canal has long been sealed off for safety reasons.

Hugh Lee Patterson of Alston invented a process in 1836 that dramatically increased the recovery level of silver. The London Lead Co. purchased the patent following successful trials at their Nenthead Smelt Mill. By 1865 Nenthead had a church, a pub, a reading room, a post office and an efficient water system that furnished a washhouse and communal baths. Sadly the lead boom was not to last. Increasing overseas competition made the venture unprofitable and in 1882, the London Lead Co. pulled out, ending their two hundred year relationship with the area.

R. W. Thornton 2002

Garrigill

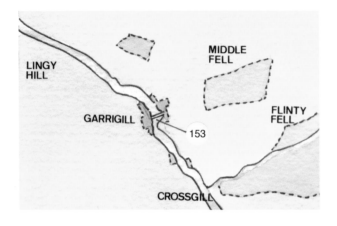

The Village Green

Garrigill lies near to the source of the River South Tyne at Tyne Head. It is an attractive village of old stone and whitewashed houses around a tree-lined green. Hidden amid the inhospitable grandeur of the surrounding moors, it is a pleasant surprise to the traveller.

Here the South Tyne flows along the easterly side of the village, confined to a rocky narrow channel and crossed by a stone bridge. Tradition has it that the river once flowed through the centre of the village and the channel was blasted out to divert the course to avoid flooding.

The tranquil setting makes it hard to believe that this was once a thriving mining community with a population of over fifteen hundred. Groups of miners would leave the village on Monday mornings to follow the trails to the mines across the desolate moors. They would carry provisions for four or five days, their destination the miners' 'shops' or lodgings adjacent to the mines. Between stints underground they would live in very crowded conditions, returning to Garrigill on Friday evenings. Life was harsh, as the old tombstones in the village churchyard attest. Infant mortality was high and many men died in their forties from 'miners lung' (silicosis) leaving widows, often with large families, in poverty.

Packhorses roped together in teams of twenty-five were used to carry the lead ore to the smelting works. They were masked to prevent them from grazing or drinking from pools along the trails, and so avoid lead poisoning from contaminated ground and water.

Miners were not averse to poaching; it became so widespread and organised that the landlord Lord Beaumont called in the eighteenth Hussars from Newcastle. The poachers literally went to ground with their weapons, concealing themselves in the labyrinth of underground workings. Reluctant to follow, the militia laid a siege, however the miners' wives successfully smuggled in food. A truce was called, with the miners' freedom in return for surrendering their firearms. However the miners substituted a heap of worthless junk. The soldiers must have realised what was happening but, fed up with their inhospitable mission, accepted and saved face.

Ashgill Force

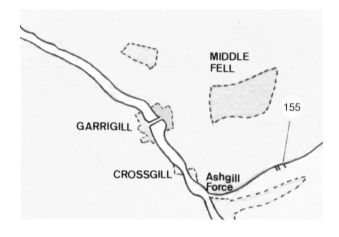

Ashgill Burn

Force is a Cumbrian word for waterfall. It is surprising that there are none on the River South Tyne itself, even though it descends fifteen hundred feet from its source on the moors to its confluence near Hexham. There are falls nearby however – at Clarigill, Nent and Ashgill. Ashgill Force less than two miles from Garrigill is undoubtedly the most spectacular.

The stream rises somewhere to the west of the South Tyne River. It is bridged by the Alston-Barnard Castle road, which passes directly over the waterfall. Countless travellers pass by without realising what a dramatic sight lies literally beneath them.

Ashgill Bridge was successfully built in 1920 after earlier attempts had resulted in collapse. Previously the stream crossing was much further upstream. Under the ridge, the fall cascades a full fifty feet over a mass of fissured limestone rock. The falls are unusual in that a path allows the careful visitor to walk behind the curtain of water where a wide shelf has been carved out. Legend has it, that it is possible to see fairies dancing.

On the bank just below the bridge was the entrance to the Ashgill Horse Level lead mine, worked in the 1820s. From here, horse-drawn wagons containing crude lead ore were brought to the 'bouse toemes' directly below the mine entrance. Bouse was the name given to unscreened lead ore and toeme was a Nordic word meaning to pour or empty (as now in 'teem with rain'). The contents of the wagons would be poured down to the stone-built bays (bouse toemes) where boys would handpick the larger lumps of ore and break up the remaining bouse with hammers before loading into a box. This box was then tilted and immersed in the fast-flowing stream, washing away the lighter rock and soil to expose the ore. It is possible to see the remains of the bouse bays.

From here the stream tumbles down the steep wooded valley creating a number of miniature waterfalls and quiet pools. The stream may be crossed by a wooden bridge built in 1992 after stepping-stones had been repeatedly washed away. The name Ashgill is probably derived from another word for a glen or dene, and from the abundance of ash trees in the area.

R.W. THORNTON 2002

South Tyne Source

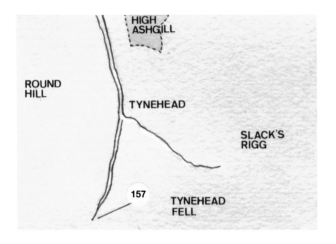

Farmstead - Cross Fell

The origin of the River South Tyne lies on the northern slopes of Cross Fell, near to the sources of the Tees and Wear and it is one of the very few Northumbrian streams that rise beyond the county boundary.

Cross Fell is just under three thousand feet above sea level and on a clear day affords panoramic views that take in Yorkshire, Durham, Northumberland, Cumbria, the Solway Firth and the North Sea. Due to a high annual rainfall such days are few and far between. The Fell can be a gloomy, damp place where, because of the nature of the ground, the rain cannot percolate but runs off into numerous rivulets towards the emerging river.

On occasion, the phenomenon known as the, "Helm Wind," adds to the bleakness of the area. This manifests itself in the sudden appearance of a line of heavy cloud along the ridge top. Within a matter of minutes the temperature plunges dramatically and a hurricane-force wind can spring up. The "Helm Wind" can last up to nine days and is especially powerful in spring and late autumn; the noise it creates can be likened to the roar of breaking seas.

Cross Fell was once more commonly known as Fiend's Fell. It was said to have been inhabited by howling demons - one wonders here if there was a link with the "Helm Wind." St. Augustine was persuaded to place a cross on the fell summit and this, together with extensive prayers, appeared to be successful in driving away the fiends who had occupied it for so long. Thus the name became Cross Fell.

Over the centuries extensive lead mining has shaped and scarred the area. A process called hushing played a principle role in this shaping process. Hushing was a method of damming water, which was then released to cascade downhill, carrying with it huge boulders and a mass of earth and small stones. As a result the soil was scoured away, leaving deep gullies and a scattering of rocks on the valley floor, which can still be seen today. The process helped to reveal new veins of ore from beneath the surface. Lead mining farmsteads were commonplace. These were usually tiny farms, often of less than fifty acres, with a barn, hayloft and living quarters all under one roof. The day-to-day business of running the farm would be left to the miner's wife and children; occasionally he would help when farming was really busy. Such enterprise enabled mining families to grow fresh food to eat; and the sale of any surplus brought in much needed revenue. Healthy outdoor work helped to counter the dangerous, health-draining conditions found underground.

Many of these farmsteads with their interlocking patterns of dry-stone walling are in evidence today and help break up the bleak and often featureless pattern of the rolling fells.

Bibliography

Land Of Singing Waters . . . . David Archer
Life And Tradition in Northumberland . . . . Frank Atkinson
Tyneside (City and County Histories) . . . . David Bean
Slaggyford and South Tynedale . . . . T. Bell
Bishop Ridley and the Reiving Ridleys . . . . Blackbull Publications
Hexham Heritage . . . . Tom Corfe
Riding Mill: A Village History . . . . Marion Cooke
The First Locomative Engineers . . . . L.G. Charlton
Hero of the North - Harry Clasper . . . . David Clasper
The History of North East Shipbuilding . . . . David Dougan
Coals From Newcastle . . . . Roger Finch
The Keelmen . . . . Eric Forster
Tyneside . . . . C.M. Frazer and K. Emsley
Blaydon Races . . . . John Gale
Highways and Byways in Northumbria . . . . P. Anderson Graham
Tynedale from Blanchland to Carter Bar . . . . Frank Graham
The Companion to Northumbria . . . . Edward Grierson
Maritime Heritage . . . . Ken Groundwater
The River Tyne . . . . J. Guthrie
A History of Northumberland and Newcastle upon Tyne . . . . Leslie W. Hepple
Northumberland . . . . Hervert L. Honeyman
Corbridge - Border Village . . . . Walter R. Iley
The Making of the Tyne . . . . R.W. Johnson
Black Diamonds by Sea (North Sea Sailing Colliers 1780-1880) . . . . David Keys and Ken Smith
Steamers At The Staiths (Steam Colliers of the North East Crossing the Tyne) . . . . David Keys, Ken Smith, Frank Manders, Richard Potts
Tyne Waters . . . . Michael Marshall
Newcastle upon Tyne Its Growth and Achievement . . . . Sydney Middlebrook
History of Hexhamshire . . . . Frederick C. Moffatt
Newcastle upon Tyne . . . . Northern Heritiage
The Tyne and Its Tributaries . . . . W. J. Palmer
150 Years of the Maltese Cross . . . . John H. Proud
Weardale, Allendale and South Tyneside . . . . J.K. Proud
Bellingham, North Tynedale and Redesdale . . . . Ian Roberts and Moira West
A History of Alston Moor . . . . Alistair Robertson
George and Roberts Stephenson (The Railway Evolution) . . . . L.T.C. Rolt
Portrait of Northumberland . . . . Nancy Ridley
Waters of Tyne . . . . T.H. Rowland
Hadrians Vale and Geordieland . . . . David Simpson
Haltwhistle and South Tynedale . . . . Tony Storey
Medieval Hautwysel . . . . Tony Storey
Built With Pride Tyne Ships: 1969-1994 . . . . Ken Smith and Ian Rae
Swans of The Tyne . . . . Ken Smith and Ian Rae
Through the Ages The Story of Nenthead . . . . Louise M. Thain
Northumberland Village . . . . Godfrey Watson

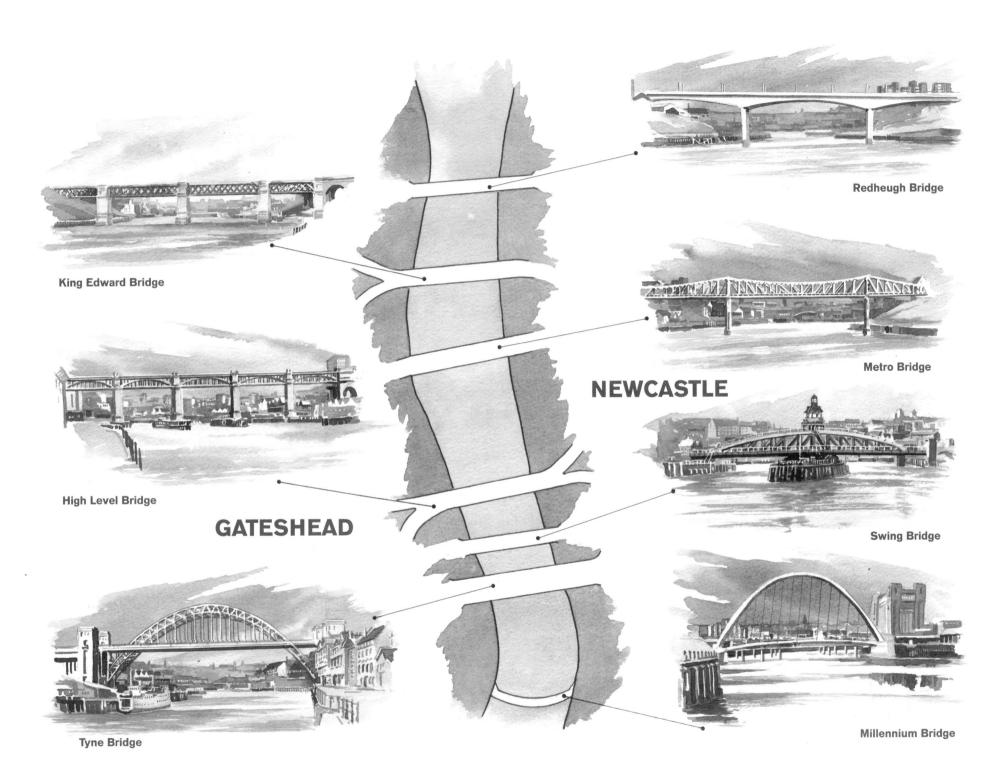

Redheugh Bridge

King Edward Bridge

Metro Bridge

NEWCASTLE

High Level Bridge

GATESHEAD

Swing Bridge

Tyne Bridge

Millennium Bridge

The last seven Tyne bridges before the sea

THE RIVER TYNE